How to Beat Burnout

For Yourself, Your Family, and Your Team

STANLEY J. WARD, PhD

ISBN: 978-1-7343937-0-5

Published by Influence Coaching, LLC
Tyler, TX
Coachingforinfluence.com

DEDICATION

To all my clients – past, present, and future:
Thank you for the opportunity to help you experience
success both at work and at home.

CONTENTS

ACKNOWLEDGMENTS

First off, thank you to my family for understanding my drive to complete another writing project.

I also want to thank two coaches who helped bring this project to life:

David Taylor Klaus – Thank you for encouraging me to choose a particular issue for my coaching to address. Working with you helped me clarify whom I wanted to help and the issues they deal with.

Kelly Epperson Simmons – Thank you helping me stay focused on the goals for this book.

To Brad Wofford: Thank you for using your design skills to create the cover and interior figures for this book.

Note – While the client stories in this book are based on the individuals I have worked with, no single story is entirely accurate in all details. Names and some details have been changed in order to protect the identities of these individuals. When put all together, these stories represent a snapshot of typical experiences for the clients I coach.

FOREWORD

"What all are you willing to let get destroyed over a fairness issue?" These are the words Dr. Ward rescued me with at the lowest point of my burnout. At that time, I had been burned out for months, had lost perspective, and was on the brink of making a series of devastating mistakes that would have negatively impacted my life, my family, my companies, and dozens of charities that those companies had been actively supporting. By calling to mind all that I was about to jeopardize by my actions, Dr. Ward helped me to realize that I had lost sight of what I truly valued. His insightful leadership enabled me to regain perspective, hit the reset button, and pull back from a burnout driven tailspin that could have otherwise resulted in irreparable damage.

After successfully navigating me through that particular crisis, Dr. Ward helped me to see that my current pace of life and way of doing things was unsustainable and was ultimately leading to the burnout that was undermining my goals for my life, my family, and my businesses. Dr. Ward worked with me over the following months to unravel the series of issues that had led to my burnout in the first place. He helped me make small but sustainable changes that enabled me to escape burnout, put guardrails in place to prevent future burnout, and begin optimizing each area of my life in a manner that was both healthy and sustainable.

Instead of trying to tackle everything all at once, Dr. Ward honed in on my greatest areas of need and helped me over time to implement many of the very same small experiments highlighted in this book. With each small experiment, I experienced incredible results in a relatively short period of time with the subtle but very powerful shifts in approach and mindset that Dr. Ward taught me. Not only was each individual small experiment a game changer for me, but when applied together with the other small experiments, they became force multipliers in rescuing me from burnout and optimizing every area of my life in a manner that was ultimately transformative and sustainable.

Dr. Ward has packed this book full of the same really powerful concepts that he utilized to help me escape my own burnout and enhance the way that I lead my life, my family, and my teams. I highly recommend this book to you if you are facing burnout personally, working with others who may face burnout, or may be susceptible to burnout as a result of the care and burden that often attend positions of leadership and responsibility. Many of the concepts in *How to Beat Burnout for Yourself, Your Family, and Your Team* also double as solid principles for enhancing leadership in general. I am confident that if you apply the concepts and tools that Dr. Ward provides in this book, you will truly be able to beat burnout and will ultimately lead a healthier and more effective life for your own benefit and for the benefit of the families and teams who depend on you.

Getting to work directly with Dr. Ward has greatly enhanced my life and my ability to lead my family and my teams for the better. In addition to helping me beat burnout, Dr. Ward has been an incredible resource to me as a consultant to work though significant business and personal transitions as well as strategic management and growth initiatives. He provides a unique combination of wisdom, experience, academic research, and a career of consulting and leadership development that work together to help people achieve effective results in both their work and family life. Much of that wisdom has made its way into this book.

I fully recommend this book as well as working directly with Dr. Ward. You will not be disappointed!

Joshua Ungerecht
CEO and Chief Investment Officer
JRW Investments, ExchangeRight, & Telos Capital

INTRODUCTION

"I'm also a client."

Let me guess. You picked up this book for one of the following reasons:

1. You feel burned out and have no idea what to do about it.
2. You feel burned out, or dangerously close, yet maintain a glimmer of hope that this condition is not permanent.
3. You feel like you are prone to burnout and want to take specific steps to guard against it.
4. You know someone who is on the edge of burnout and hope this book can help.

If any of those made you nod, then this book is for you. I know firsthand the effects of burnout, and I also know it doesn't have to be a lifelong condition. In the following pages, I share how you can beat burnout and continue to do demanding work without depleting yourself. Life can be fulfilling and rewarding without costing you your health, your family, or your career.

"Please talk with my husband." I heard these words

from a concerned spouse after she listened to one of my presentations on beating burnout. The gentleman I was introduced to was affable, but also upset. Don's employer was asking more and more from him. In fact, it was more than Don wanted to give. Unfortunately, he still had at least ten years until retirement. Quitting now was not an option. What was Don to do?

This example is not unique. In a world of continuing and rapidly increasing change, where "hustle" is the key to success, a number of high achievers are finding themselves feeling increasing pressure, and unsure of what to do about it.

Believe me, I've been there. If you grew up in the 1980's, you may remember a commercial for the Hair Club for Men where the spokesperson said, "I'm not only the president. I'm also a client." The same is true for what I present here. I've had my own struggle with burnout, and I continue to proactively manage it daily. In these pages I'm not only writing about burnout; I'm also my own client. (And for the record, I would not be a spokesperson for the Hair Club for Men. If you've seen me speak or spotted my bio photo, you know I haven't worried about regaining any hair loss. But I do care about beating burnout.)

Those of us who perch too close on the edge of burnout know all about putting too much pressure on ourselves. Coming from an academic background, I sometimes feel the need to be research-heavy, but I have found that when it comes to burnout, the answer is not just more information. We don't need to read one more study; we need to grasp the concepts that can help us right now and put them into play.

Instead of "breakthrough research," I want to deliver well-tested information and practices that work well for a specific type of person. If you are still reading, you most likely are that person. (Or perhaps are married to that person.)

Have you ever really thought about what burnout is? If

you've seen *The Princess Bride*, there is a wonderful quote: "I don't think that word means what you think it means." To avoid that problem here, I provide definitions and examples of burnout from both trusted sources and from my own experience (which will hopefully become a "trusted source" for you as we spend time together). We will dive into the three dimensions of burnout, and I will offer ways to beat these burnout indicators. After all, that is our goal here.

What I find to be most helpful for making changes in life are what I call "small experiments." Don't be misled by the title, small experiments can generate a big impact. For each dimension we identify, you are given small experiments to apply in your own life. Results can be immediate – and can last a lifetime.

By adopting the paradigm shift that comes with practicing small experiments, you will discover that you can still do significant work in the world without self-immolating.

This is my wish for you: be a high-caliber person doing good work in the world without the high levels of chronic stress and exhaustion that lead to burnout. It is absolutely possible. Let's get started and begin that work together. Like I said, I'm not just a leadership coach who helps high achievers beat burnout, I'm also a client of my own practices.

CHAPTER 1

YOU ARE NOT A SLACKER

"This book is not for slackers."

IN THIS CHAPTER, YOU WILL DISCOVER

- Who this book is for
- Four questions to help you know if you are teetering close to burnout
- Who else burnout impacts

AM I TALKING TO YOU?

As a leadership coach, I've been blessed to work with a variety of hard working, talented, brilliant people who deeply care about both the missions of their organizations and the people who carry out that mission. I've worked with both for-profit and nonprofit leaders in industries as diverse as aerospace, automotive sales, community development, finance, and even organizations fighting homelessness. For all leaders who are doing good work for good reasons – in any industry – you need to sit up and pay attention.

Why? You are at risk.

"This book is not for slackers." What do I mean by that? My clients are driven people who have a constant sense that "I need to be doing more ..." Does that sound like you? If you feel like you always could do/should do a little more, you aren't a slacker. Indeed, you are the opposite.

I'm writing this to help those who are most likely to burnout, not the "slackers" in an organization, but those who genuinely care about getting results and who also work hard to make that happen. This book is for those people who have so much to offer to their organizations, communities, friends, and families. My hope is that by following the guidelines here, you will avoid burning out and robbing those same organizations, communities, friends, and families of all you have to offer.

You are not a slacker. Rather, you are someone who, simply by reading this book, is deciding to push back. You understand burnout is a very real threat to those who want to do good work in the world. Slacker? Absolutely not! If anything, you are choosing to be a proactive role model who both gets things done and does it in such a way that you, your family, and your workgroup all benefit.

To find out if this book is *really* for you, see if any of this sounds familiar:

- You value hard work.
- You are wired to over deliver.
- You care deeply.
- People depend on you.
- You feel the weight of your role.
- For you, there is more on the line than financial profit. You care about the lives of the people your decisions impact.
- You care about both results and relationships (by the way, effective leadership requires both – so congratulations on having this motivation!).
- You want to be a contributor in the world and not just a consumer of stuff.
- You want to be strong so you can also strengthen others.
- You value personal growth for the sake of service to others and not personal benefit alone.
- You are a high achiever.
- You want to develop leadership skills that will help move yourself, your teams, and your family as far from burnout as humanly possible.
- You are ready to drive a stake in the ground and live a life of core commitments.
- You want to take action and make change wherever you can.

Any of that ring a bell? Then read on

PERSONALITY TYPE

Folks who are interested in coaching work are also often interested in personality assessments. For example, if you've done the DiSC personality assessment, you may find yourself to be a high "D" or a high "C." My clients who seem most prone to burnout often display one or both of these personality traits.

The "D" type is a driver and doer. You are often motivated by challenge and a drive to control situations and (sometimes) people. You want to prove yourself to the world — showing that you can handle difficult situations and make things happen. While this personality type can serve you well, and probably has already — the drive for control and achievement, as well as a tendency not to notice feelings, can lead to some of the burnout factors we are trying to avoid

The "C" type is highly conscientious, focused on demonstrating competence as well as often being compliant. Like the "D" type, you are task oriented, but more motivated to "get it right" rather than just to "get it done." Because you can be detail oriented, you don't like being rushed to complete assignments. This personality type has benefitted you of course, and some may see you as either especially reliable or an expert. Super. And these default behaviors can also push you toward the negative end of the burnout spectrum.

The D and C personality traits can be like a superpower for you. However, if not managed properly, they can also become your kryptonite (for my readers who missed out on comic books, that is the one substance that can harm Superman).

Even if you have never done a personality assessment, you may know that you are a driver, a doer, a get-it-done-perfectly kind of performer. This is not about changing who you are or how you are wired. This is about recognizing when you are on the path to burnout and what you can do to circumvent it.

When I first met Janet, she was restless. It had been a particularly taxing year in her organization. Relationships were strained, hard decisions needed to be made, and Janet was feeling ineffective at getting things done – or more to the point, more things needed to get done than she could ever do. She didn't want to leave her organization, but she knew something needed to change in order for her to stay. Janet began asking herself hard questions about her work and her relationships. Are you starting to ask yourself questions as well?

FOUR IMPORTANT QUESTIONS
To prepare the ground for our work together, let me ask you four questions. Then read the sample responses. If the questions and responses resonate, or some of your own immediately pop to mind, then you are ready to do the work in these pages.

What change do you want to see in your life?
- More energy at work and home
- More joy
- Better relationships with peers and family
- Sense of accomplishment from work rather than dread

How will you know you've achieved such change?
- At the end of the workday, I'll have the energy to do something besides crash on the couch
- My stomach won't churn when I arrive at work
- I'll actually want to listen to what my coworkers and direct reports have to say
- I won't feel like I have to do it all myself
- At the end of the week, I'll feel like I've actually accomplished something

What resources will that make available for you?
- Energy to go do something after work with friends or family
- A greater sense of achievement at the end of the workday
- Improved relationships at work and at home

What's the cost of doing nothing?
- My health suffers
- My enjoyment of life, work, and family decreases
- The people I really care about get the worst of me instead of the best
- I stop functioning as a high achiever
- I stop caring about work

WHY SHOULD YOU CARE ABOUT BURNOUT?

All of the above. If you do nothing about burnout, your health, relationships, and zest for all areas of life can plummet. Neither the people you love nor the mission that matters will get the best of you. Continuing on full steam ahead and ignoring the warning signs can do more harm than good. You want to do good – that's why you work so hard. You care. You have passion. You have so much to contribute to your organization, community, friends, and family. They need you. The world needs you. You can be a leader in all these spaces – inspiring and transforming them. But if you don't take burnout seriously, you are going to deprive both yourself and all these people of the amazing gifts you have to offer.

You are the type of person I like to work with, as a colleague or a client. The world needs your input and impact. My work in the world is to come alongside you, to keep you from falling prey to burnout (due to your own good intentions), and thus ensure that the people who need your contributions the most receive them.

The more intentional you become with how you

manage yourself, the more you are able to give all of your talents to the causes and people you most care about. This might seem obvious, but taking of yourself may not be at the top of your to-do list. The term "self-care" often makes hard-working high-achieving leaders recoil in horror. Guilt enters the picture or you think your time is better spent working on your projects rather than taking a few moments for yourself.

This thinking is going to have to change.

When you think of self-care, do you cringe and look for something "productive" to do? To borrow a phrase, "Well, there is your problem." (And it is my problem too.) The term "self-care" brings up mixed feelings for many, because it can feel "indulgent." I'm much more comfortable thinking about how to meet the needs of others instead of the "wants" of myself. (See what I did there – it's hard for me to even discuss my "needs.")

Let's address that right now. If you are a top performer who is motivated to serve others, it is easy to get so focused on the work you want to do that you forget an important fact – *you* are the primary tool for accomplishing that work. And as every craftsperson knows, you've got to take care of your tools. If you were a woodcutter, you would sharpen the axe that made your work possible.

Self-care is not about selfishly treating yourself and ignoring the needs of others; it is about taking care of yourself precisely so you are able to address the needs of others.

Note the change of words here. You address the needs of others. Feeling like you have to "meet" or "solve" the needs of others is also part of what leads to burnout.

So, let's motivate your self-care. This is about self-care that also benefits others. It is not "selfish." Proper self-care is about taking care of yourself so that you can help others in a way that allows your impact to be more effective and sustainable over the long haul.

REAL WORLD EXAMPLES

Will gave 150% in every area of life, except self-care. He was committed to his organization and team and mission, his family, his church, even his lawn care at home, but he did not commit to his own self-care. He thought his time was better spent taking care of everything and everyone else. He was an "always on," "get it done" kind of guy, until one routine checkup, when he discovered that he was putting himself at risk for a stroke. In order to stay alive, he had to make serious changes. Will realized that if he were a saw or a knife, he had worked the blade until there was no bite left to cut. Think of self-care as routine maintenance for equipment. Regular attention keeps the tools in tip-top shape.

As a personal example, my wife was in a car accident and sustained a brain injury several years ago. She lost her ability to work and take care of family responsibilities for a time. I was working full time and also working on my PhD in leadership studies. Add to that taking care of my wife and our two young daughters made my full plate feel overloaded, and I struggled to manage it all.

This went on for over a year. I'm competent, capable, compassionate, and self-reliant. I kept telling myself I could do it all. But I was wiped out. I found myself spending most of my time feeling angry. One day I had the realization of what I was modeling for my daughters. I didn't like it one bit. If it were true that my daughters would grow up to marry someone like their father, I didn't want that for them at all. I didn't like the current version of me, and I certainly didn't want them to marry someone who was angry all the time. So, I made time to work on me – not just for my sake, but for the sake of my family as well. I realized self-care was not a luxury, but instead critical to take care of all the responsibilities I had.

You too are devoted to your family, your team, your

organization, your mission, and your life goals. You are not "self-absorbed." You are externally focused. This is exactly why you need to learn how to beat burnout.

Please repeat after me: "Self-care is not selfish."

Now we can go to work.

CHAPTER REVIEW

- If you are zealous (in a good way) about your work and your life, you may be at risk for burnout.
- Some personality types are more susceptible than others.
- The cost of ignoring burnout – doing nothing – will impact you, your career, and your family.
- Take care of yourself so you can take care of all that matters to you.

CHAPTER 2

WHAT IS BURNOUT?

"I'm exhausted, disconnected, and ineffective."

IN THIS CHAPTER, YOU WILL DISCOVER
- Symptoms of burnout
- Consequences of burnout
- Professions that tend to be more susceptible to burnout

SO, WHAT IS "BURNOUT"?

"Burnout" can be a slippery term, and it is one that shows up in conversations regularly. Have you heard this from friends or family or thought it yourself?

- "I'm burned out at work."
- "I'm burned out at school."
- "I'm burned out at home."

So, what exactly is this malaise that seems to be so common?

Let's start with this: burnout is about more than just being tired. We naturally go through cycles of exertion and recovery. Burnout is about getting stuck at the halfway point in the cycle where there is only exertion and no recovery. It's about being tired and lacking the resources to recharge

One illustration I can give is for you to try this: make a fist, as tight as you can. Now hold that for a few hours. How will your hand feel afterward? Can you use it to get much done? Probably not. You may find that after a certain period of time, you can no longer make the fist. Or, you may feel like your hand locks up and you can't release it. Even though you've let off the pressure, your hand still won't function. Burnout is a similar experience.

Others have described burnout as "compassion fatigue," or the inability to care anymore.[1] When you think about the number of things calling for your attention and "care," that fatigue makes sense. We similarly know that "decision fatigue" affects those who have to make lots of decisions, so it only makes sense that those who care about a lot of things could experience a similar compassion fatigue. And that fatigue can express itself in a variety of ways. I suspect the anger I mentioned earlier was an example of me running out of the ability to care, no longer motivated by positive emotional states like compassion and empathy. Instead, I relied on anger as a source of energy for getting things done.

Think of burnout as facing ongoing and increasing demands with decreasing resources until those resources are so depleted that the system stops functioning. The world needs you to keep functioning and to do so in a healthy way. People who experience burnout are givers. So to avoid burnout, you have to learn to give to yourself as well. Then you can be at your most effective when you give to others.

The World Health Organization (WHO) focuses on burnout as an "occupational phenomena" rather than a medical condition, though it can certainly influence a person's health. According to the WHO:

> Burnout is a symptom of chronic workplace stress that has not been successfully managed. It is characterized by three dimensions.
> - feelings of energy depletion or exhaustion;
> - increased mental distance from one's job, or feelings of negativism or cynicism related to one's job; and
> - reduced professional efficacy.
>
> Burn-out refers specifically to phenomena in the occupational context and should not be applied to describe experiences in other areas of life.[2]

While the WHO may emphasize that burnout is primarily work-related, I'm interested in how it impacts people's personal lives as well. For me, it's hard to draw a strong dividing line between my personal life and my professional life. When one is doing well, I experience the benefits of that in the other. And in the case of burnout, the opposite is true as well – when one is overtaxed, it impacts the other. That's why our work together here is so important. We truly have only *one* life.

Maybe it's silly to title a chapter on what burnout is, since honestly, no one has ever asked me what burnout is. Many of us feel like we experience it. We know intuitively that something is wrong. What we need is to treat it, or better yet, prevent it.

WHAT IS THE COST OF BURNOUT?

Burnout creates "waste" in individuals, organizations, and families because of the potential contributions it steals from all these groups. Who pays that price? You and those you care about.

Wasted resources aren't the only cost. The consequences of burnout can be numerous. Mayo Clinic and the Maslach Burnout Inventory suggest this list of problems related to job burnout:

- Excessive stress
- Fatigue
- Insomnia
- Sadness, anger or irritability
- Alcohol or substance misuse
- Heart disease
- Type two diabetes
- High blood pressure
- Vulnerability to illnesses
- Inability to regulate negative emotions[3]

WHO EXPERIENCES IT?

Some of the most troubling discussions around burnout have involved physicians, which has been labeled "a public health crisis" because of its impact on both individual physician's mental health and by implication, the well-being of all those they treat as patients.[4] Nearly half of all physicians report some form of burnout.

Anyone in a "caring profession" or "service profession" is at risk, and that includes ministers, teachers, counselors, healthcare workers, social service workers, fire fighters, police, emergency medical services, and the list goes on and on. Given the rise of customer service measurements for those in business, anyone in sales or management can also experience the factors of burnout. It does not matter what profession – administrators, nonprofit leaders, CEOs, middle managers, executives – or industry. If you feel responsible for your work product and those affected by it, you may be a candidate for burnout.

If you put in long hours, no matter how well compensated, you still feel high demands and you want to meet or exceed goals or expectations. You have a certain pride in your work. Layer in the demands of being a parent, spouse, caregiver to aging parents, community volunteer, whatever else you have going on in your life, and it is no surprise that burnout occurs.

Burnout scenarios are everywhere.

- Consider the lawyer who already works over 60 hours during the week and often needs to do additional work on weekends just to keep up. This professional goes to annual reviews with the firm where the message is not "thank you for your hours," but rather "how can you give us more hours and increase the firm's income?"

- Consider doctors who previously had help with record keeping and transcription of their notes. Now these highly trained professionals are expected to keep records as well as treat patients, so they put in an additional one or two hours a day with electronic medical records in addition to their long hours of patient care. Plus, there doesn't appear to be any relief in the near future.

- Consider the increased pressures felt by university administrators as their schools become more and more dependent on tuition at a time when the college-going population of traditional students is shrinking. These administrators can't control generational birthrates or swings in the economy that impact families' ability to afford college, yet they are still accountable for filling programs with successful students

The consistent message professionals receive:

- Do more.
- Do it faster.
- And, use fewer resources.

That external pressure is tremendous, and it is made even more intense by the internal drivers of those who push themselves to work hard. Perhaps you take pride in over delivering. At one time, that deep passion and commitment to results was a superpower – but now it has become your kryptonite that can lead to burnout.

YOU ARE NOT ALONE

Dean came to me because of complaints that he was too volatile during professional meetings. I had worked with Dean before, and I knew he was genuinely concerned for both his company and his staff. So here was a talented go-getter who seemed to be sabotaging himself. Dean knew he needed help because workplace stress was also affecting his health. His family was frustrated because he could never put down his phone if someone called or texted after work hours. Dean realized he was not in a good emotional or mental state, and simply told me, "I can't keep going like this."

We've all had experiences with varying degrees of burnout in life. Exhaustion, discouragement, and even a growing detachment from the people around you are warnings that you need to make changes. Burnout can involve different contexts, different symptoms, and different responses.

Sometimes we feel it physically, sometimes emotionally and mentally

I certainly have. At one point, I was so stressed at my job and working such long hours that I stopped sleeping at night. This was going on when my wife was pregnant with our first child. In a different scenario, I had received some negative feedback at work and was not enjoying my job. I was quickly losing my sense of purpose and needed to do something about it. In a third example, I ended up in the ER with an obstructed bowel for no obvious medical reason. Later we realized that it was an extreme stress response. While that third experience wasn't strictly workplace burnout, all three of these experiences had one thing in common: the realization that "I can't keep going like this."

So I didn't. I sought help.

In the first case, we were expecting a child and I knew that I was going to be useless to my spouse because of mix of chronic exhaustion and sleeplessness. I worked with a counselor and I decided to change jobs.

In the second case, I had been in the process of looking for a new career path and felt myself disengaging from my current work more and more. When I began to get negative feedback about my work performance, I didn't have a backup plan of where I could work next. I hired a coach to help me reconnect my core strengths and interests to my work and looked for other opportunities to better align what I did on a regular basis with what I really cared about.

The third case had the most extreme symptoms. When we couldn't find medical solutions in Texas, we went to the Mayo Clinic in Rochester, Minnesota for two weeks of diagnoses, which were eventually followed by another two weeks of therapy. That therapy included both physical therapy and training in self-care to help me moderate my stress responses. It's my stress responses that I continue to work on today, and why I am able to work effectively with others who are stress magnets. (Been there. Done that.)

Because I'm driven for achievement and productivity, I

have learned how to give myself permission to rest on a regular basis. I've also learned that I don't have to over deliver on every project (which used to be a real point of pride for me). Previously, in order to be "responsible," I felt like I had to be "always on." Now, when I find myself feeling like I have to go-go-go all the time, I recognize that as a warning sign. In response, I intentionally slow down.

My leadership coaching work has now expanded to include beating burnout because I've found that we generally coach best what we need most. Because of my experiences with burnout, and because I continue to self-monitor for it, I am able to help others out of that mess. I want to help others beat it – and hopefully *before* they end up in a hospital. If you have thought, "I can't keep going like this," you're right. You can't. But there is something you can do about it.

CHAPTER REVIEW

- Burnout can express itself in a variety of ways and impact you both at work and at home.
- Burnout creates waste – in potential and contribution.
- Anyone can be susceptible to burnout and its symptoms.

NOTES

1. See Compassion Fatigue Awareness Project. (n.d.). What is compassion fatigue? Retrieved from http://www.compassionfatigue.org/pages/compassi onfatigue.html

2. World Health Organization. (28 May, 2019). Burnout an "occupational phenomena": International classification of diseases. Retrieved from https://www.who.int/mental_health/evidence/burn -out/en/

3. Job burnout: How to spot it and take action. (n.d.). Retrieved from

https://www.mayoclinic.org/healthy-lifestyle/adult-health/in-depth/burnout/art-20046642   See also, Maslach, C., Jackson, S., & Leiter, M. (2018). *Maslach Burnout Inventory Manual.* Retrieved from www.mindgarden.com

4. Jah, A. K., Iliff, A. R., Chaoui, A. A., Defossez, S., Bombaugh, M. C., & Yael, Y. R. (2018). *A crisis in healthcare: A call to action on physician burnout.* Retrieved from Massachusetts Medical Society and Harvard Global Health Institute website: https://cdn1.sph.harvard.edu/wp-content/uploads/sites/21/2019/01/PhysicianBurno utReport2018FINAL.pdf

CHAPTER 3

SMALL EXPERIEMENTS

"Always be experimenting"

IN THIS CHAPTER, YOU WILL DISCOVER
- Beating burnout is a process
- The power of small experiments
- The importance of becoming a reflective practitioner

PREFACE NUMBER ONE: "CAVEAT EMPTOR"

Before we start our work together, I need to offer a few prefaces. The first is this: let's get clear about what I'm offering you. The phrase "caveat emptor" is a Latin phrase that translates "buyer beware." In other words, it's the buyer's responsibility to make sure what she is buying really will meet her needs and is of the quality she expects. Whenever you buy a used car marked "Sold as is – no warranty," you (hopefully) practice *caveat emptor*.

Likewise, before we get to the nitty-gritty on how to move away from burnout and toward something much better, I need to offer a disclaimer. If you are looking for a book that tells you the solution is to drop out of life and go live on a resort island for six months, you are going to be disappointed. My goal is to provide you with tools and skills that will help you beat burnout in the daily grind of life at work and home. In the process you may realize that you need to go spend six months in a resort location. If that is the case, cool. Enjoy it. (Send me a postcard, please.) Just know that we aren't starting with that option.

I also need to offer some good news and some bad news.

- The good news: you really can beat burnout.
- The bad news: Just reading a book won't do it for you. You have to implement what you read.

Another disclaimer here – I don't want to dismiss the numerous systemic challenges that lead to burnout. Sometimes you may need to leave that system in order to beat burnout. What I'm doing here is working under the assumption that we should strive for the "minimal effective dose" in your situation, rather than going for an "amputation" to address a wound that could heal in other ways

Think of the minimal effective dose as the difference between boiling water at 212 degrees Fahrenheit versus boiling water at 400 degrees Fahrenheit. Both can get the job done, but the second option uses up way more energy than was required. Another illustration is the "quick start" instructions you find when opening a new electronic device. The short foldout pamphlet is like a minimal effective dose for getting the device up and running versus trying to read the entire instruction manual. Both the pamphlet and the instruction book provide you with useful information, but the "quick start" focuses only on what is essential.

While writing this book, I came across another example of a minimal effective dose, this time regarding exercise. We hear a lot about 10,000 steps as a guideline for health, but fewer steps can still be beneficial.[1] Don't get me wrong. If you can do 10,000 steps, great! However, you may not need all that in order to get the health results you want.

Oh, and don't stress out trying to find the exact "minimum" required. Just know that sometimes doing less than what you are used to is just right.

PREFACE NUMBER TWO: "DO NO HARM."
Now that we are clear on what I'm offering you. Let's talk about how we are going to do that work together with a "first principle." First principles are the fundamental concepts that serve as a foundation for a theory or model. In our work together beating burnout, we have a first principle as well:

First, do no harm.

You've probably heard that phrase before as part of the famous Hippocratic oath taken by doctors. In a sense, we are working together to help you become a doctor who can "heal thyself" (to borrow another famous phrase) so it only makes sense that "do no harm" is part of how this whole deal works.

The activities suggested in this book are meant to be beneficial behaviors and mindsets that can lead to measurable positive change. The key here is to use these tools in such a way that they fulfill their intent rather than causing problems. Let me illustrate from my own life.

Tai Chi, the Chinese martial art practiced for defense training as well as health benefits and meditation, has been a blessing for both my wife and me. However, because of my drive to over deliver and prove myself, I nearly injured myself early on doing an exercise form that is noted for being injury-free and even ideal for octogenarians!

In the first few classes, I kept pushing my movements beyond what others were doing, thinking this would make me stronger. Instead, I was actually extending myself to poses that were less stable and putting strain on muscles and joints that true Tai Chi actually protects. After a few sessions of this, I called the training center to ask about why my knees hurt so much and if I should take a few weeks off.

The response: "Um, I've never heard of this before. Tai Chi is supposed to make things feel better. I've never known someone to injure himself while doing Tai Chi."

Please learn from my experience. Don't "burn out" while trying to beat burnout. (It's embarrassing. Trust me here.) Over delivering on these small experiments is counter-productive. Don't do it.

OUR PROCESS: SMALL EXPERIMENTS

One of the ways we can "do no harm" is by following a process of "small experiments." Let me explain: the goal for beating burnout is not to "do more." Instead, it is to "do different."

If you've been in sales, you are probably familiar with the expression "ABC" or "Always be closing." For our work together, repeat after me: "ABE" or "Always be experimenting."

One of the core principles in this book, and one derived from my personal experience, my work with clients, and even my academic work, is the power and value of "small experiments." Small experiments involve a commitment to a *specific* action over a *limited* timeframe. Add to that an extra commitment to re-evaluate the actions taken and make changes if needed. The biggest advantages for small experiments are that you don't have to get it right the first time and even when uncertain, you can still make progress.

Here are some things to keep in mind.

- **You don't have to get it right the first time.** This feels contrary to how most conscientious leader types want to work. But the problem of trying to always get it right on the first attempt is that you often feel the need to delay action while waiting for more information. So small experiments are a tool for when you don't have all the information, but you still need to make a decision. The freedom to not get it right the first time is also a boon for those driven toward proving themselves through high achievement (which can then turn into a counter-productive kind of perfectionism which then leads us to burnout). We aren't keeping a scorecard here and penalizing you for making mistakes. Instead, we measure how much you *learn* from experience and how you apply that for your future benefit.

- **Even when uncertain, you can still make progress.** This follows from the point above. Once you are clear on the goal, even if your action doesn't produce the result you want, you still make progress. How? Because you've found an option that doesn't work and you can cut it from the list of other possibilities. To illustrate: I can't help but think of an apocryphal story about Thomas Edison. He supposedly said, "I have not tried and failed 1,000 times. Rather, I have found 1,000 ways that don't work." To repeat: the focus here is to learn and then to apply what we learn in our situation.

- **Small experiments help you take back your power.** As the burnout experience becomes more intense, we can feel more and more like victims of our situations. (At least, that's been my experience.) Part of the value of small experiments is that they give you an opportunity to make deliberate and informed decisions. You can take actions of your own choosing. That way you are not simply a victim of circumstance.

While they may not sound like a "big deal," small experiments are powerful. They allow you to minimize risks when trying new things. And, when you share about what you are learning with your family and your work team, they all benefit. Key point here: in the same way that experiencing burnout can impact these people negatively, you can also have a positive impact on them by the way you chose to beat burnout and share the process with them.

Let's return to my mention of Tai Chi so you don't overextend yourself like I initially did when learning to practice it. Tai Chi is a kind of "moving meditation" that emphasizes gentle, flowing movement. While non-competitive, it still provides benefits by stretching and strengthening core muscles at your own pace.

Similarly, our small experiments are not competitive, and you go at your own pace. There are differing styles so you can do it your way and not worry about keeping up with anyone or comparing yourself with anyone else. Like Tai Chi, our small experiments will focus on:

- Slow and deliberate movements, emphasizing fluidity and not getting "stuck"
- Not overextending yourself
- Being highly self-aware at first, which then becomes "muscle memory" over time

And that "muscle memory" thing leads me to my next point with small experiments.

CHANGE TAKES TIME

Give yourself three months minimum to see results. In both my coaching work and teaching work, there is just something about that three-month mark. My shortest coaching programs are three months long, and in that time we can see tremendous results. I generally recommend a six-month commitment to help make those changes really stick (and we will talk about "reinforcement" later). Likewise, in my teaching work at a university, I supervised action research projects of approximately three months in length. It is amazing to see the unanticipated results at the end of that short time when we have a laser-focused goal to pursue. After three months of intentional small experiments, we can start to see some big changes. So ask yourself, "Where do I want to see big changes in the next three to six months?"

The purpose of this book is to help you clarify where you *want* to make change and provide you with suggested small experiments to help you make change. If you don't *desire* to change, the change won't happen. I'm borrowing here from a change model by Prosci, called the ADKAR model.[2] ADKAR is an acrostic for:

A = Awareness

D = Desire
K = Knowledge
A = Ability
R = Reinforcement

While the model was originally developed to address changes in organizations, I find these concepts to also be helpful for *personal* change.

According to the model, resistance to change can be assessed in a linear progression. What I mean by that is, if there is no awareness, then no reason to change. Likewise:

- If there is awareness but no desire, then no change.
- If there is awareness, and desire, but no knowledge, then no change.
- If there is awareness, desire, and knowledge, but no ability (or skill), then no change.
- And finally (here is what most often gets left out by managers in a change initiative) if there is no reinforcement for all of the above, then the change won't stick.

In writing this book, my goal is to address all five parts of the change model to help you beat burnout. In particular, the last chapter deals with "reinforcement" because it is so important and yet so easy to overlook.

Part of that reinforcement, by the way, is to *reward your successes.* Because I demand excellence from myself, it's easy for me to ignore what I'm doing well and only give attention to the failures.

Several years ago, I tried mountain biking as a hobby. Trail biking is different from road biking because the paths are so incredibly narrow and there are so many obstacles to address. I found myself falling quite a bit. Then a friend pointed out that I was naturally steering toward what I was paying attention to. To stay on the path, I had to focus on that path and quit staring at the obstacles I *could* crash into. Otherwise I *would* crash into them.

Similarly, if we want to reinforce our successes, we have to pay attention to them. One way to do that is to celebrate them. We will look at this in detail later. While we may not be able to change your exact situation in three months, we will most definitely change how you approach that situation, and your approach makes all the difference.

Here is an example of changing how you approach a situation. When clients feel particularly stuck, I've found one coaching exercise to be particularly helpful. I ask the client to imagine who they want to be in 20-30 years and describe that person in detail. We talk about the perspectives and wisdom of that person as well as what they have accomplished. Then, after their "best self's" motivations and character qualities are clear, I ask the client how that person would approach this issue. The shift in perspective can be profound.

For example: during a coaching call Susan was really stuck. She had a clear goal. Unfortunately, every time we discussed that goal, she found herself saying over and over "I don't know how to do this." We changed her approach when she asked for her best self's perspective. When she looked back on the challenge facing her from the perspective of her future self, here are the words that quickly came to mind: "I did this!" Once we made that paradigm shift, Susan was convinced change was possible. Then she was able to work backwards and develop a plan of action.

At the end of your three to six months of experiments, you will find yourself with a new set of knowledge, attitudes, and skills that will transform your experience of daily life and that includes how you experience yourself, your team, and your family.

SMALL EXPERIMENTS VERSUS "JIMMY BIG LEAGUE."

A popular chewing gum product at the local grocery store when I was growing up was "Big League Chew." I can still remember the cartoony, exaggerated batter on the cover (in purple, because grape flavor was my favorite). I call that guy "Jimmy Big League," and he is the part of my personality that is always swinging for the fences. He's certainly helped me be successful in some spaces, but he can get in the way of small experiments because he will overcommit and do *way more* than the minimal effective dose.

So the secret here is to pick out just one or two small experiments to start with. Focus on learning, and then reward yourself just for doing the work. One of my favorite coaching principles from the Co-Active Coaching model is to "deepen the learning and forward the action." Small experiments help us do that because they focus on taking action as a small experiment and then reflecting on the action so we understand our situation better and then make adjustments for next time.

Another problem for Jimmy Big League (who I suspect is responsible for some of my original injuries when I started Tai Chi) is that he feels the need to "max out" and do "max reps" whenever possible. This is a bad idea when you are struggling with burn out because you are already "maxed out." Small experiments are a space where you make real progress when you do just 1-2 repetitions of an exercise you've never done before.

If Jimmy Big League starts talking in your head, tell him to go to the dugout. That joker is contributing to your burnout. Later we will learn how to give him a focused purpose so he helps you instead of hurts you.

BECOME A REFLECTIVE PRACTITIONER

In part of my work as an educator, I teach graduate students how to become reflective practitioners. Watching them develop their skills in this area is a treat – partly because I continue to experience benefit from reflective practices in my own life. To do small experiments well, you need to become a reflective practitioner.

Reflective practice tells us that we don't learn from experience alone, but rather from thinking critically about our own experiences. And, the quality of those reflections can determine the quality of what we learn. Reflective practitioners are able to observe their current situations, form a hypothesis of what an improvement could look like here, try an action, and then learn from the results. Then they repeat those actions with new insights, starting the loop over again.

Coaching is about both listening and challenging. The process I ask you to take here is to "listen" to yourself while reading the book – what do you become aware of that you didn't realize before? How does this change the way you look at your situation? Then challenge yourself by choosing at least one small experiment to apply that insight.

I first learned to become a reflective practitioner when I was certified to be a ropes course instructor in the 1990s. After moving participants through a series of challenging experiences, we would stop to reflect on those experiences and how those insights could be applied to both their personal and professional lives with three questions.

- What?
- So what?
- Now what?

These questions take a look at what happened, consider the significance of what happened, and then consider how to apply that significance to future situations. Essentially, you ask yourself, "Based on what I've learned from this present experience, how will I chose to act differently in the future and what will be the value of that action?"

As a coach, I see myself as helping clients become reflective practitioners while I act like a Sherpa. My goal is to walk beside you while we climb to the top of the mountain for insight and clarity. Then we return to the base of the mountain for application and action taking.

As we move forward in this book, I ask that you visualize the mountain climbing experience. At the end of each chapter, what gets clearer to you? How can you act on that knowledge? When we reflect that way, we "deepen the learning and forward the action."[3]

Reflective practice will serve you well when you want to become a person who changes their approach to a specific set of circumstances. When applying reflective practice, the specific details of your situation may not change, but your approach to it does. That new approach makes all the difference.

From now on, we will pause at the end of each chapter for you to experience reflective practice by asking yourself questions about what insights you've gained from each chapter and how you can apply them for yourself, for your family, and for your team.

In my coaching work, I've had multiple opportunities to coach senior leaders while their organizations were "right sizing." Often our conversations would address the inevitable stresses these managers faced as they made decisions that affected both their organizations, the lives of those employed by their organizations, and the families of those same people. For leaders who care deeply and push themselves to work hard, moving an organization through a time of layoffs can be crushing. To help these managers cope, our conversations helped them become reflective practitioners where they paid more and more attention to their internal and external responses to the various challenges of that season. They weren't able to change the market realities that challenged their business, and they weren't able to change a situation where they had to lay off staff – sometimes people they had worked with for years. What they were able to change is how they approached a difficult situation, and they were able to move through it in a way that kept themselves from self-sabotaging while also giving hope to others.

ANOTHER KEY IDEA: NEUROPLASTICITY

You may be aware of neuroplasticity: the brain's ability to reorganize itself by forming new neural connections throughout life. Research shows that our brains have the ability to change – to strengthen or even create new synapses. Consider these small experiments a way to impact your brain's neuroplasticity so you can beat burnout!

With each small experiment, you are testing skills and ideas that you can then continue to repeat as they serve you well, and in the process of doing all this you are literally retraining your brain. These small experiments will serve as "brain exercises" to help you approach your situations with new attitudes and skills.

Beating burnout is not just about "will power" or learning new tricks. Beating burnout is learning a new way of being – a different way of operating that is both beneficial and sustainable for you. And, it all begins with small experiments.

CHAPTER REVIEW

- Understand that small experiments have large impact.
- Watch out for Jimmy Big League!
- Become a reflective practitioner to deepen the learning and forward the action.

FOR REFLECTION

- What's something new that you discovered about beating burnout?
- How can you apply that insight for yourself?
- How can you apply that insight for your family?
- How can you apply that insight for your team?

NOTES

1. Aubrey, A. (n.d.) 10,000 Steps a day? How many you really need to boost longevity. Retrieved July 6, 2019 from https://www.npr.org/sections/health-shots/2019/05/29/727943418/do-you-really-need-10-000-steps-per-day
2. What is the ADKAR Model? Retrieved from https://www.prosci.com/adkar/adkar-model
3. I first came across this phrase from Co-Active Coaching. See www.coactive.com

CHAPTER 4

BURNOUT AND FIGHT OR FLIGHT

"Paper tigers vs. real tigers."

IN THIS CHAPTER, YOU WILL DISCOVER
- The relationship between our fight or flight response and burnout
- How to get out of fight or flight
- A core skill for beating burnout: "Breathe and Big Picture"

THOUGHTS ON "FIGHT OR FLIGHT" AND BURNOUT

The "fight or flight" response is how our body responds to a perceived threat. When we believe ourselves to be in danger, our body tenses for action and our pulse quickens. Our breathing becomes shallower. If you are in a situation where you need to fight to defend yourself or quickly run away, this bodily response prepares you for that. It is an automatic response. We don't have to tell ourselves, "Oh, it's time for me to quicken my heart rate so I can get out of here."

Notice I said "perceived" threat. The trick here is that sometimes what we think is a threat is a non-issue. As one of my clients likes to say, it's about "paper tigers vs. real tigers." So the problem is that when we think there is a threat (and it really isn't one), we go into the same tense state, and we respond to a situation as if we really were in danger. Our brain gets a massive dose of hormones and the end result is what Daniel Goleman, author of *Emotional Intelligence*, calls an "amygdala hijack."[1] In other words, the fight or flight response takes over no matter what the situation really is. If you've ever experienced an anxiety attack, you have a good sense of just how bad that hijacking can get.

The other problem is that our bodies were not made to stay in "fight or flight." Instead, our bodies need to spend ample time in the "rest and recovery" state so that we can digest food and repair any damage to our body. When we spend unnecessary time in the fight or flight state, we do ourselves more harm than good and deny ourselves the rest and disconnect needed to keep burnout at bay.

GETTING OUT OF FIGHT OR FLIGHT

For the leaders I work with, getting out of a state of "fight or flight" is one of the biggest factors to address. A classic illustration of this can be found in nature (or your favorite nature documentary) where a predator of your choice (lion, tiger, or bear – oh my!) stalks, chases and nearly catches a prey of your choice (antelope, bunny rabbit, or nature hiker). At some point, the prey is able to escape his predator. What's fascinating to watch is how the prey is able to "shake off" the experience (following the wisdom of Taylor Swift) as if nothing had happened.

What fascinates me about this is how different it is from my own experience of "near misses," or worse yet, the amount of time I spend dreading hypothetical near misses. We are trained to look for danger, and I suspect that much of the advertising that bombards us is trying to convince us that we are in lack or in danger of missing out (FOMO is real). We also have 24/7 newsfeeds that constantly feature worst-case scenarios. All of this can provoke that fight or flight response, when there is no real predator nearby.

One of my clients, Hank, found himself constantly stressed when he interacted with peer managers at his workplace. When we dug into his situation, Hank realized that he was constantly seeing these peers as "threats" rather than as "co-workers." Once he changed how he perceived these peers, Hank's stress at work decreased noticeably.

Stanford psychologist Emma Sepella explains fight or flight works well in small doses, but there is a real cost and danger to staying in that state for more time than necessary – resulting in anxiety, a variety of nervous system disorders, and yes, burnout. She points out, "If you are able to stay calmer throughout the day, you'll have energy for when you really need it."[2] In other words, when we keep Jimmy Big League on the bench, he'll be ready to do his job when bases are loaded. Otherwise he will wear us out.

The challenge for me, and for those who are wired like me, is a tendency to depend on fight or flight energy too much. We rely on that rush of energy to move through work and challenges in life, whether those really were fight/flight worthy or not. And when we spend more and more time in fight or flight, we are not resting and recovering. Spend too much time operating that way, and some form of burnout is inevitable.

So, part of both my client work and my own learning has been to distinguish between "paper tigers" and "real tigers" and to find different energy sources for dealing with paper tigers.

"BREATHE AND BIG PICTURE"
When I catch myself relying on that fight/flight response to do work, I then make the adjustment to "breathe and big picture." Essentially, the fight/flight part of the brain and the "big picture" part of the brain don't operate at the same time. It's one or the other.

So, repeat after me: "Breathe and Big Picture."

The goal here is to help us spend more time in the parasympathetic state (rest and digest) rather than the sympathetic (fight or flight). As a conscientious high achiever myself, I look at that goal and say, "Right. You don't get it. 'Rest and Digest' doesn't get stuff done." And if that is your objection, you are correct to a point. If *all* you do is rest and digest, then you won't get stuff done. However, because rest and digest does promote healing and refueling for our bodies, it allows us to then get more stuff done in the longer run. (Remember the story about sharpening the axe?) Looks like it's time to repeat a phrase from earlier in the book: *Self-care is not selfish.*

Please understand, I'm not advocating living in a constant state of rest and digest. Instead, I am advocating skills that help us not get stuck in fight or flight. In other words, we want to make sure we move back and forth between the two states with self-awareness. When we are staying in fight or flight, let's make that an intentional and informed choice. When we stay in rest and digest, let's likewise make that an informed and intentional choice for the sake of a specific goal. Think of this as learning how to intentionally go into work mode, play mode, or rest mode.

In the Human Resources work I've done with leadership coaching projects, I've never been called in because a leader spends too much time in the "rest and digest" state. Instead, I have been called in because the otherwise amazingly talented leader spends too much time in "fight or flight" and the results were derailing their career.

Many of my clients are highly driven and competitive by nature. When something gets in the way between them and their goal, their natural instinct is to crush that resistance or run over it (the "fight" in fight or flight). The problem here is that when that resistance comes from an employee, if the leader is not self-aware, he will treat that co-worker like an obstacle to be crushed or run over rather than a colleague with a differing opinion. That is *not* effective leadership.

Let it be known that being "calm, confident, and content" is not a threat to achievement. Many driven, passionate leaders struggle to accept that at first. Yet, as they notice their thoughts, actions, and behaviors, they find themselves even more effective at warding off the factors that lead to burnout. With increasing self-awareness, they build skills in being more calm, confident, and content while still getting stuff done.

The first experiment we will try, before we even dig into anything else, is "breathe and big picture." Once you can do this with intention, you are ready to take on the other small experiments.

Another reason we are committing to small

experiments is that we want to do work that does not cause such stress that we trip the fight or flight response. You may find that trying something new feels awkward, and you might even feel less effective at first than you were before. That is ok. In fact, it is to be expected.

As an illustration, consider what it would be like to learn to write with your opposite hand. If you are right handed, imagine the process of learning to write with your left hand. At first, your work would be slow and messy – much less effective than just using your "normal" hand. However, after a season of practice and pushing through the dip in performance, you would find yourself able to do a pretty good job with that hand – effectively doubling your writing capacity and providing some margin should you right hand get injured in some way.

Please note that there is a difference between something feeling awkward at first and something actually causing pain. So if any of these experiments cause pain, stop doing it and try something else.

Diaphragmatic Breathing

Some experiences are so fun and exhilarating that they take our breath away, like a great ride at an amusement park. Other experiences induce panic and leave us feeling like we can't breathe. High achievers often experience both.

For example: one week after successfully defending my dissertation and earning my PhD in leadership studies (an exhilarating experience), I ended up in the hospital with severe intestinal and digestion problems and later received a dire-sounding diagnosis (stressful enough to take my breath away).

Dissatisfied with my diagnosis and lack of treatment options, I went to the Mayo Clinic for more tests for a second opinion. The major issue appeared to be a chronic stress response I had developed. What I discovered through diagnosis and treatment procedures was that, among other things, I wasn't breathing right.

Let's process that a moment – how many of us pay attention to how we breathe?

While we may not pay much attention to that specific behavior of breathing, when we don't do it right we experience all kinds of complications. For me, I allowed the combined stresses of studies and work, along with other curveballs in life, to "take my breath away." That response was interfering with my ability to do things we otherwise take for granted (like eating). As part of my treatment, Mayo taught me the benefits of things like mindfulness based stress reduction, Tai Chi, and even how to breathe correctly.

In my coaching work, I've found that as leaders continue to deal with stressful situations, they also can forget how to breathe correctly. Here is the basic idea:

- Inhale through your nose, and *slowly* exhale through your mouth.
- Put your hand on your belly and your chest. With deep breathing, you should feel your belly move and not just your chest.
- Repeat just two or three times in a row at first – preferably while sitting down. If you do it too much, you may get lightheaded.
- Whenever you feel yourself in fight or flight, respond by thinking "breathe and big picture." That will help you use the logic part of your brain instead of the fight or flight part. Diaphragmatic breathing also helps. Once your heart rate calms down, you are ready to do the strategic leadership work.

Believe it or not, I've read how the military teaches a similar method to help troops focus when they come under fire. In a world of "do more, faster" the ability to intentionally slow your heart rate will serve you well.

As a fascinating side note, deep belly laughs can

produce a similar response as deep belly breathing, so feel free to include humor in your small experiments. Sometimes laughter really is the best medicine.

"Big Picture"

The fight or flight response focuses us on immediate concerns – those which feel life threatening. In this state, our body tenses, our breath becomes shallower, and our vision narrows. The problem here is that what may seem like "immediately" beneficial is not necessarily so in the long run. When you are uncomfortable dealing with a co-worker, you may want to run away from the conversation or feel the need to put that person "in their place." While those actions might seem to provide some sort of immediate sense of release/relief, you are not addressing the main issue that can cause even more problems later.

The idea with "breathe and big picture" is to remove yourself from the emotion of the moment and pull back to see the situation more objectively. What truly is the big picture goal? After you take a few deep breaths as described above (breathe), ask yourself "What do I want this relationship/situation to look like six months from now?" (Big picture.) Now you are able to see more options and can begin to do what makes that overall desire possible.

All our small experiments are specific expressions of "breathe and big picture." In fact, if you will simply spend one week on just this "simple" behavior, you will start to see benefits in moving away from burnout and toward something better.

Another big picture exercise is to see the perceived threat as just a *part* of life instead of the *whole* of it. When I'm overly stressed about a particular challenge, my wife asks me to tell her three things I'm grateful for. At first, I'm annoyed because I feel like I'm being distracted from the issue (and I am – but that is the point here). However, that exercise helps me put the challenge into a much larger perspective of all the good things in my life, which then helps me "shake off" the threat that in reality is a paper tiger.

You can start applying this technique today. Spend one week paying attention to when you find yourself in fight or flight. When you catch yourself, think "breathe and big picture."

CHAPTER REVIEW
- You can learn to monitor your fight or flight response.
- Living too long in fight or flight leads to burnout.
- You can calm that response with "breathe and big picture."

FOR REFLECTION
- What did you discover about fight or flight?
- How do you apply that to beat burnout for yourself?
- How do you apply that to beat burnout for your family?
- How do you apply that to beat burnout for your team?

NOTES
1. Goleman, D. (1995). *Emotional intelligence: Why it can matter more than IQ.* New York, NY: Bantam Books.
2. Schoenberg, N. (n.d.). Stanford psychologist tells us how to fight workplace burnout. Retrieved April 13, 2019, from Chicagotribune.com website: https://www.chicagotribune.com/lifestyles/sc-fam-work-burnout-remedy-family-0405-20160309-story.html

CHAPTER 5

THE THREE DIMENSIONS OF BURNOUT

"Burnout is not the same as worn out."

IN THIS CHAPTER, YOU WILL DISCOVER
- The three dimensions of burnout
- The Maslach Burnout Inventory (MBI)
- Burnout is a spectrum

MORE THAN "JUST TIRED"

We all get tired. And we all know that burnout is more than just being tired. Burnout is not the same as worn out. If that were the case, a weekend of R&R would put you right back on even keel. What I've found that works well with my clients is to label the three dimensions that can be used to measure a person's burnout: emotional exhaustion, depersonalization, and ineffectiveness.

In the following chapters, we'll define each of these dimensions and give concrete examples. We'll also talk about the *opposite* of those dimensions so you can visualize that state for yourself and express it in your real life. Then, we will start our small experiments for beating burnout.

While it may be tempting to skip right to the small experiments, you need to start with doing the awareness-building work of knowing what to look for in your own quest to beat burnout. You'll start by learning what to avoid and then determine what you want to pursue.

Until you know the direction you really want to go, you won't know if you are truly making progress. After all, "movement" is not the same as "progress" because we can move *away* from our goal without realizing it. (Consider those times where a confused football player triumphantly runs the ball into the wrong end zone.) Before you choose a small experiment, you need to determine if it is a "best fit" for the change you want to see in your life.

THE MASLACH BURNOUT INVENTORY

When I decided to address burnout as part of my coaching work, I looked for a research-based assessment that could help me measure burnout, and I quickly came across the Maslach Burnout Inventory (MBI).

The MBI was first published in 1981 and is "recognized as the leading measure of burnout." It has been administered to thousands of people and has been tested for both its validity and reliability. The MBI focuses on "causes and outcomes of burnout, but is not a clinical diagnostic tool." One benefit of the MBI is that it can help us recognize factors that contribute to burnout in our own lives and take corrective action.

Originally concerned for human services workers like doctors, nurses, teachers, and police, as the research developed, the researchers realized that burnout impacts people across a number of occupations. Essentially, anywhere people are engaged in "intense activities," there is the chance of burnout taking place.[1] No surprise there.

What the MBI Measures
The MBI defines burnout as a combination of three types of feelings: emotional exhaustion, depersonalization, and low personal accomplishment, which can also be labeled "ineffectiveness."

Burnout is not an "on" or "off" experience, but rather a spectrum of feelings – low, medium, or high. When I first started studying burnout in earnest, this insight of burnout as a spectrum of experiences was significant to me because it meant that all of us are on this scale somewhere. As a coach, my desire is to help people (a) become aware of where they are, (b) make an intentional choice about where they want to be, and (c) provide support in getting them there. If you are still reading this book, you are probably somewhere on this scale and want to move to a better place.

In a conversation with Malcolm, a university administrator, I mentioned my coaching work on burnout and Maslach's three dimensions. As I described the dimensions and how to address them, Malcolm leaned in with increasing interest. After a pause in the conversation, he leaned back in his seat as a realization kicked in.

"I was burning out, and I didn't realize it." Malcolm went on to describe an intense season at work that left him physically exhausted. He thought a vacation would solve the problem. Yet, when he returned from vacation, he found himself no better off.

What surprised Malcolm was that although his vacation did not seem to revive him, after a few weeks working on specific, *meaningful*, projects, his energy began to come back. How is it possible that he could be energized by meaningful work when his vacation did not seem to do the trick? Keep reading to find out.

EXTERNAL PRESSURES VS. INTERNAL RESOURCES

When external pressures exceed internal resources, then a system begins to collapse. For our purposes, burnout happens when external stressors continue well past the point where internal resources are able to resist those stressors. My goal is to help you increase your "internal resources." In the example above, meaningful work helped restore those internal resources more effectively than simply taking a vacation.

The process here is to develop habits, behaviors, and ways of thinking that continue to push back against burnout *before* one is completely burned out. The sooner you start these new habits, the better. Recovery from full burnout can be a lengthy process. Anyone who is both driven to produce results and driven to genuinely care will benefit from applying these small experiments, no matter where they are on the burnout spectrum

Maslach called for more research on the interventions that help reduce these negative emotional states and their consequences, and our "small experiments" are just that – personal research done by reflective practitioners that will both reduce the negatives and increase the positives.

So, what are you doing to intentionally increase your internal resources and/or decrease external pressures?

In the following chapters we will take a look at each of the three factors and the small experiments you can use to beat them. As stated in the beginning of the book, the idea here is not to "do more," but to "do different."

CHAPTER REVIEW

- The Maslach Burnout Inventory (MBI) is a tool for measuring the causes and outcomes of burnout.
- Burnout is a spectrum of experience and not "on" or "off."
- Three measurable dimensions of burnout are: emotional exhaustion, depersonalization, and ineffectiveness.

FOR REFLECTION

- What did you discover about the three dimensions of burnout?
- How can you apply that insight for yourself?
- How can you apply that insight for your family?
- How can you apply that insight for your team?

NOTES

1. Maslach, C., Jackson, S., & Leiter, M. (2018). *Maslach burnout inventory manual.* Pp. 1, 74. Retrieved from www.mindgarden.com

CHAPTER 6

BEATING EMOTIONAL EXHAUSTION

"I'm tired of being tired."

IN THIS CHAPTER, YOU WILL DISCOVER

- What emotional exhaustion is, what it looks like, and the costs
- What the opposite looks like
- Small experiments for beating emotional exhaustion

AN INTRODUCTION TO EMOTIONAL EXHAUSTION

Chris had worked tremendously hard to take his struggling organization from a state of decline into a place of stability, and now even to a season of prosperity. Yet in spite of that success, he found himself still working long hours and feeling constant pressure to keep the organization in that place of prosperity. Chris feared that if he ever let up, the organization would quickly sink back into that place of near implosion that he found it in when he started his leadership role there years ago. He felt like he was out of gas and did not know what to do about it.

Emotional exhaustion goes beyond being tired. For some, it's a weariness that goes to the soul. Simple rest can help with physical exhaustion, but this is something bigger than what can be fixed in a weekend off (though taking time off is a good start when you begin to feel this way).

Maslach suggested that emotional exhaustion is a significant beginning of the burnout process, and Monique Valcour explained that this exhaustion is caused by a number of factors:

- An always-on culture that runs 24/7
- Intense time pressures
- Having too much to do
- Not being able to control work
- Disliking work
- Lacking the skills to accomplish work

With the result that "previously enjoyable tasks seem arduous, and it becomes difficult to drag yourself both into and out of the office." [1]

For anyone wired with excessive dedication and devotion, emotional exhaustion is a risk, especially because the way we push ourselves to be "all in" with work can mean that we create additional pressures to perform besides those already present in the situation. While running at "full bore" may have been your superpower previously because it helped you stay out in front of problems and gave you the stamina to work longer hours and get the results you wanted, there comes a point where that backfires. Your amped up ardor is no longer fuel, but instead kryptonite. No longer feeling fired up, you feel emptied out with no reserve fuel.

As we continue "giving it all we've got" day after day, our physical and emotional energy resources become tapped and we don't give ourselves the space needed to restore those sources. Even worse, we may find ourselves running full throttle in the wrong direction because we've not taken the necessary time to reflect on the big picture of the situation and make sure we are pursuing what is best for all involved, including ourselves, our families, the teams we lead, and the overall mission.

What Emotional Exhaustion Looks Like
Defining things in behavioral and observable terms is helpful. In my coaching conversations on beating burnout, here's how emotional exhaustion has been described to me:

- Reactivity
- Anger
- Shut down
- Waking up in the morning and not wanting to go to work
- Having no extra energy after work when you get

home
- Drinking to cope with stress
- Wanting to be alone after work instead of spending time with family
- Insomnia
- Chronically missing the emotional energy needed to do good work
- Loss of passion and drive
- Overwhelm
- Irritability
- Physical collapse
- Anxiety
- Panic
- Shrinking
- Self-Medicating
- Depression

The phrase "running on empty" is exactly what is going on here. Life demands a lot from high achievers in terms of physical, mental, and emotional energies – and all three of those are important. When one of those gets low, we start compensating in counterproductive ways, which can then drain our resources even further.

Think of a car engine. That engine needs a lot of resources to run well. Gasoline is an obvious one, but it also needs oil as a lubricant to keep the parts from breaking each other. Think of emotional exhaustion as a car engine that is running out of *both* gas and oil, yet still trying to run. How long is that going to work?

As a father to teen drivers, I've made a point to teach them the dangers of driving a car that is low on oil. Likewise I want to warn you about trying to drive yourself with only fight or flight energy when entering burnout. The results are not pretty.

The Costs of Emotional Exhaustion

Part of my research for this book included interviewing people about their perceptions of burnout in their workplace. One lawyer observed that sometimes new lawyers started out bright and strong, working long hours with enthusiasm and always delivering a great work product. Then, a change would occur. Their work became consistently late and of low quality. The observer realized this was the first warning sign of a young lawyer approaching burnout. One of the easiest ways to recognize emotional exhaustion at work is to indeed look for a noticeable change.

But what if that highly productive and highly engaged person at work is you? Are you able to discern a change? Do you see the costs?

My client Ron stepped into a demanding leadership role in his organization. It was a new space, and one he was excited about. However, as time went on, the job demanded more and more from him both physically and emotionally, until the only emotions he had left to run on were the darker ones – especially anger and worry. Yes, Ron could still run on that emotional fuel, but it took a toll on him, the team he led, and the family he came home to.

Running that engine on empty is going to cause things to break, and they are going to be expensive to repair. When my well-used car's engine continued to leak oil and was going to need an engine replacement a few years ago, I realized that it would be better to replace the whole car instead of just the engine. What's your emotional engine look like? Does it need a replacement, a new fuel source, or basic maintenance?

Don't get yourself in a situation where the easiest solution is just to replace you.

WHAT'S A HEALTHIER ALTERNATIVE?

Knowing what to avoid is good, but just avoiding the "bad

stuff" is not exactly a motivator for sustainable change. I'm reminded of a religious observation that sometimes people spend more time and energy "running away from sin" rather than "running toward righteousness." Simply thinking, "don't burn out," is not enough. What do you want to be running towards? Being proactive rather than reactive is key.

So what then is the "do" that we need to do? To figure that out, we return to the idea of burnout as a spectrum of behaviors and experiences. Imagine a 10-point scale. At one end of the scale is "Emotional Exhaustion." We've already listed some of how that manifests. What words or phrases would you choose for the opposite of feeling emotionally exhausted, at the other end of the scale?

Your ability to define the *opposite* of emotional exhaustion in clear, behavioral, experiential, measurable terms is your first step to beating it.

One of the blessings of my work as an educator and coach is that I get to work with a variety of motivated people who strive to make a positive difference in our world. Early in my research on burnout, I shared the idea of emotional exhaustion with a friend who is one of these kinds of people. Tina is the CEO of a large non-profit doing significant work. The conversation was going in a typical manner as I explained the concept of emotional exhaustion and the burnout spectrum. We were both in a logical, factual mode, and she was curious about the information. Then I paused and said, "OK, now define what the opposite of emotional exhaustion is for you."

At that point, Tina paused. She became quiet and introspective, and the emotional energy of the meeting changed. She looked at me with reddened eyes and said, "Stan, I can't even imagine that."

I hope that is not your internal dialogue as you read these words. If it is, let me help you imagine the opposite of emotional exhaustion. Here is a list of words suggested by coaching clients and research. Which of these words resonate with you? Instead of emotionally exhausted, would you rather feel:

- Energized
- Passionate
- Both relaxed and focused
- Encouraging, appreciating, showing gratitude
- Motivated
- Content
- Happy
- Fully Present
- Productive
- Engaged
- Joyful
- Abundant
- Hopeful
- Creative
- Strong
- Animated
- Fresh
- Lively
- Refreshed
- Restored
- Vigorous
- Open
- Day one of a startup
- Emotional energy to share
- Wide margins
- Peaceful
- Doing fun things
- Growing intellectually and spiritually
- Having energy after work to enjoy friends and family

- Having energy/resources to pursue a hobby

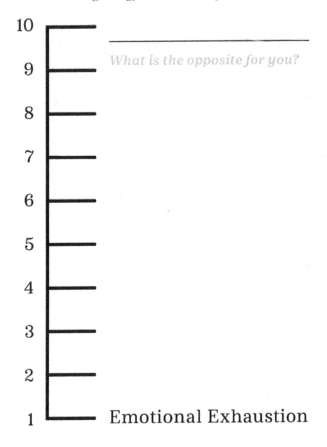

What is the opposite for you?

10
9
8
7
6
5
4
3
2
1 — **Emotional Exhaustion**

The point of thinking through the opposites here is to create a target for you to shoot for. In fact, the clearer you are on what that ideal state is for you, and the better you can name it in both emotional and behavioral terms, the better chance you have of achieving the goal. Remember, we are running toward something positive and not simply away from something negative.

One reason for this greater likelihood of success is that when you are clear on the outcome you wish to achieve, it will be easier for you to determine the right small experiments for getting there. Also, you can't know that you are making progress when making a change unless you can tell that you are getting closer to a particular goal. Otherwise you are just making movement (which might cause even more exhaustion if you are not intentional).

Now, let's motivate that goal a bit. If you experienced two or three things on that list, what would it make available for you? What's that worth to you?

SMALL EXPERIMENTS FOR GETTING THERE

Emotional exhaustion is a major predictor for burnout. When you feel yourself moving into this space of emotional exhaustion, it is time to take action.

You ask: "What can I *do* about burnout?"

My answer: start with small experiments.

To start, remember the general principles for small experiments:

- Do no harm.
- Follow cycles of action and reflection.
- Give it time.

To beat emotional exhaustion, focus on two things:

- Rest
- Recharge

Because emotional exhaustion is such a significant predictor for burnout, we have a longer explanation of experiments here than for the other two factors.

Small Experiment Set #1 – Rest

You may be thinking, "You've got to be kidding me! I bought your book on beating burnout and you tell me to "rest?!" I knew I needed that – it's why I bought the #$% book!"

OK, I get that feeling. I had that same feeling myself when I was at Mayo and they started with "Tell me about how you relax." My first thought was: *The best medical minds want me to "relax"? Are you kidding me?*

But it's because of that Mayo experience that I'm starting with rest here. So let me ask you now: "How do you relax or disconnect?"

Rest Both Mind and Body. Endlessly watching YouTube videos is not the same as rest. While our bodies may be still and lying prone, our minds are staying active and we are being bombarded with stimuli. At Mayo, I learned that resting is about quieting the mind and the body at the same time.

Note that the question asked by Mayo was "how do you rest or disconnect?" In other words, true rest is not just about physical rest or a lack of physical activity (so "rest and recharge" can also include, and probably should include, exercise). It's also about how we get our *minds* to rest – and that has become increasingly difficult in an era of always-on phones that deliver instant alerts for news, emails, and your cousin's latest rants.

So "breathe and big picture" here means taking time to breathe and disconnect. We start by giving ourselves space for rest, even if it is only for a few moments.

Let's return to some of our discussion about fight or flight. The more time you spend in the "rest and recover" space as compared to fight or flight, the more rested and recovered you will be. We are not talking about living in rest and recover. No, instead we want to train ourselves (a) to get back to rest and recovery as soon as possible when we find ourselves in fight or flight and (b) to keep ourselves from needlessly living in fight or flight.

For some people, this is easier than for others. If you find yourself stuck in fight or flight, it doesn't mean you are "weak." It just means your central nervous system has been hijacked. We are going to take back control. Here are some ways to do that.

- **Experience Sabbath.** One consequence of a 24-7 society is that we've lost touch with the value of concepts like "Sabbath." You don't have to be a religious person to appreciate the value of taking one day a week to focus on things like rest and reconnecting with something much bigger than yourself. Both of these are important for beating emotional exhaustion because we need both physical and spiritual fuel to make that happen.

- **Unplug.** Symptoms for burnout include the inability to stop thinking about work or the sense of our muscles being constantly tense. It's like we are an electrical appliance with a broken "off" switch. If we don't want the appliance to run, what do we have to do? We have to unplug it. For some clients, to unplug means completely disconnecting from the phone or computer for a 30-minute lunch break. For others, it means giving themselves permission to have "non-productive" time on the weekends. For me, it means scheduling time on Saturdays to rest in my hammock and read a good book, away from my electronic distractions.

Slow down your heart rate. Many of my leadership clients find themselves under constant pressure. Note that I say "pressure" here and not "stress." The Center for Creative Leadership explains that there is a real difference between the two. Pressure is unavoidable, but we experience negative stress when we ruminate on those pressures with regret and anxiety. To correct this, we must "wake up" from that rumination.[2] One way to wake up is to connect to something that is observable in the present moment – like our breath or heart rate.

Sometime during coaching calls, I hear clients' voices

quicken and I can feel the rising emotion on the other side of the phone. When that happens we pause to notice what is going on. (Notice how noticing is a theme here in these small experiments?) Sometimes, just the act of "noticing" helps take the edge off. Other times, we stop and practice deep breathing until the client can feel his heart rate slow.

Sometimes our hearts and minds race because of a particular kind of rumination – fighting hypothetical battles. For example, I'm a highly conscientious type who likes to be prepared. So I sometimes imagine every possible critique of the work I'm doing, or every possible way something could go wrong.

"What's wrong with that?" you may ask. "You are just being thorough."

Not exactly. What I'm doing to myself is putting myself in a fight or flight state multiple times a day when there is no real threat present – only a hypothetical one. When you find your heart racing as you think about possible scenarios, you are no longer just "planning ahead," you are ruminating anxiously.

Use the minimal effective dose. This one is especially important for overachievers. In effect, we want to find the amount of energy needed to get the job done, and not contribute more than that. If one tap of a hammer can pound in the nail, there is no sense in beating it 500 times. Think about the amount of wasted energy for the same result. It's the same thing here. This concept is especially appropriate for those of us wired to over deliver.

I know I am not alone in my tendency to want to over deliver. I have an annoying habit of offering to deliver results in the shortest realistic time possible. You say you need it by the end of the week? I'll try to deliver it in 24 hours. When I pull that off, it makes me look amazing. (Or so I think.) However, when I can't get it done in that reduced amount of time, I find myself needing to ask for permission to deliver "late." I'm stressed, because of a *self-*

imposed timeline that was not necessary in the first place.

What motivates a need to over deliver? It can be a desire to prove your value to the client or organization, as well as a desire to continually be ahead of the "need curve" so that you are predicting needs and addressing them before they come up. That's one of the things I evaluate myself on. The problem here is that I'm not omniscient. I can't always predict the need. How do I handle that? Sometimes by feeling guilty with an increased need to work even harder and faster. And the downward spiral to burnout begins.

In both my own leadership journey and with many of the clients I work with, I hear an idea that "If I were a better leader, we would have fewer problems." Here is where our conscientiousness or drive is really at work. While there are some problems that a careful leader can avoid, the reality is that we work in communities and organizations that are often addressing what can feel like unlimited needs with limited resources.

Instead, look at it this way: it's precisely because of these issues that we need you to show up as a leader. Instead of seeing every blip as a threat to your leadership and/or employment, embrace it as job security by virtue of how you handle the situation. When you show up as a strong and capable leader, does it help calm nerves and energize spirits? Then use that as your success metric rather than critique yourself for an unanticipated problem.

Small Experiment Set #2 – Recharge

What do you do with a battery that has used up its energy? You have two options. If it is a standard battery, you may simply throw it away. On the other hand, if it is a rechargeable battery you can bring it back to full strength, and it is powerful again. People can be like that. When we allow ourselves to get depleted and don't take any intentional actions to recharge ourselves, we may feel like we are throwing our lives away. Thankfully, there are things we can do to intentionally recharge.

Schedule activities/conversations that energize you. During one of my coaching sessions, Judith described how her week was full of meetings that drained her. As we continued talking, she was able to identify a few relationships that were both professionally beneficial and recharging. We created an action item for her to intentionally schedule at least one of those energizing meetings a week. These meetings allowed Judith to be both productive and recharged instead of constantly depleted.

Practice learned optimism. This model was created by Martin Seligman, as an alternative to a state described as "learned helplessness" – when we feel like no matter how hard we work we aren't able to achieve our goals.[3] With learned optimism, we take intentional steps to counter the things that drain us by thinking about them differently. His model is wonderful in that it can be explained simply like this:

- A = Adversity. Something bad happens to you.
- B = Belief. You then make a judgment about yourself or the world you live in.
- C = Consequence. When we have negative beliefs, we experience negative consequences. We can find ourselves drained of optimism and hope if we stop here. And that is what happens with learned helplessness. However, Seligman's model takes two more steps.
- D = Disputation. We can challenge that belief – not by simply thinking about fairy tales and unicorns, but by doing an honest reality check and reframing the situation.
- E = Energized. The result of challenging those negative beliefs is that it energizes us.

Here is an example of what that can look like.

- A = Adversity. You work in a constantly changing environment in a growing organization and a lot is demanded of you. When the organization was smaller, you could easily predict problem areas and solve issues before they became problems. Now your organization and responsibilities have grown to a point that no matter how well you try to plan ahead, unexpected problems happen. You can no longer create bulletproof solutions.
- B = Belief. "I must have lost my edge and I'm no longer an effective leader."
- C = Consequence. Self-doubt. Growing despair. Loss of confidence and enthusiasm for work.
- D = Disputation. Instead of thinking the problems prove your ineffectiveness as a leader, see the problems as evidence that your leadership is needed. These are opportunities for you to show your value as a leader.
- E = Energized. Now when problems show up they are not a threat because they are not evidence that you are ineffective. Instead, they are a call sign like the "bat signal," meaning the organization needs you to show up as the qualified leader you are.

Bringing Rest and Recharge Together
Sometimes you can combine rest and recharge through hobbies or exercise. Activities like running, bicycling, fishing, golf, yoga, or whatever floats your boat (as the case may be) are helpful. Another popular way to experience rest and recharge in shorter doses is the practice of mindfulness. Mindfulness is a discipline where you work to gently quiet the thoughts that distract you and focus on the present moment for a set period of time.

Sometimes our minds are like a small pond of water where the silt on the bottom has been stirred up, and the water looks like a mess. However, if the water is allowed to stay still long enough, the silt settles back to the bottom and the water becomes clearer. There are a variety of apps now to help you with this. I use Headspace and have found it very helpful.

Another metaphor I use when working with leaders is that of a diesel engine. I ask them to think about how a diesel engine is able to pull tremendous loads, yet it does so at low speeds and without going into high RPMs. By doing so, the engine experiences less stress; it lasts longer; and, it is still powerful.

What it would be like for you to work like a diesel engine?

CHAPTER REVIEW
- Emotional exhaustion is the strongest predictor of burnout.
- The opposite of this factor includes feeling energized, passionate, relaxed and focused.
- Small experiments for beating emotional exhaustion include rest and recharge.

FOR REFLECTION
- What did you discover about emotional exhaustion?
- Which of the small experiments made the most sense to you?
- How can you apply that experiment for yourself?
- How can you apply that experiment for your family?
- How can you apply that experiment for your team?

NOTES

1. Valcour, M. (2016, November). Beating burnout. *Harvard Business Review.* Retrieved from https://hbr.org/2016/11/beating-burnout

2. Petrie, N. (2014). *Wake up! The surprising truth about what drives stress and how leaders build resilience.* The Center for Creative Leadership. Retrieved from www.ccl.org

3. Seligman, M. (2016). *Learned optimism: How to change your mind and your life.* Vintage Books: New York, NY.

CHAPTER 7

BEATING DEPERSONALIZATION

"I just don't care anymore."

IN THIS CHAPTER, YOU WILL DISCOVER

- What depersonalization is, what it looks like, and the costs
- What the opposite looks like
- Small experiments for beating depersonalization

INTRODUCTION TO DEPERSONALIZATION

James received feedback that he needed to be more collaborative, so he strove to do that – inviting team member opinions, working to listen more, being more open and honest in conversation. Yet when times got hard for the organization, his team seemed to become even more critical of his work. After months of this, James found himself more cynical about his teammates and about leadership in general. He felt an increasing distance between himself and his staff, and he didn't know what to do about it. This disconnect is an example of depersonalization.

The *Maslach Burnout Inventory Manual* explains that depersonalization can also be described as "cynicism," or when we feel disconnected from both our work and/or our co-workers. This disconnect can be harmful for those who want to make a positive difference. In order to have that kind of impact, you have to be willing to get close and to take the risks that go with closeness. That was the struggle James was facing. Thankfully, he was aware of it and took action to work on it.

Often depersonalization follows on the heels of emotional exhaustion. After all, it is only natural to want to protect yourself when you feel like people and projects suck you dry. One of the ways we do that is by distancing ourselves and withdrawing from those people and projects.

What Depersonalization Looks Like

Let's return to the illustration of the hand that's been balled into a fist and squeezed for too long. While you make a fist, you are not able to hold anything or shake someone's hand. Once you finally get release from that fist, do you want to use that hand to do anything? No. That's what depersonalization does. You feel a bit numb and want to keep that hand "disconnected" from both work and relationships. You withdraw for self-protection. That's what depersonalization feels like.

Now let's think about this in terms of "superpower" vs. "kryptonite." Our superpower of working hard and caring deeply helps us:

- Connect because we care
- Extend ourselves for the sake of others and the mission of the organization
- Experience fulfillment as we connect our personal values to the values of the organization

That superpower becomes kryptonite when:

- We care so much that we find ourselves constantly hurting
- We've extended ourselves so far that we withdraw in order to self-protect
- We find a mismatch between what we care about and what is being asked of us at work

When I speak with clients about what depersonalization looks like in their own lives, this is how they describe it:

- Pulling away from everybody
- Having only a small group of friends and losing them
- Passive aggressive behaviors
- Withdrawing behavior
- Unproductive conflict
- Binging on Netflix

- Prone to distraction
- Avoiding relationships
- Angry and impatient
- All task focus and no relationship
- Panic when tasks aren't completed
- Reclusive
- Disconnected
- Cynical
- On Autopilot
- Procrastinating
- Lack of Sensitivity
- Saying "I don't care."
- Isolating
- Saying "Let it burn."

Obviously, this doesn't feel good. At an HR conference I had the chance to discuss this concept and attendees quickly began to identify team members who didn't seem to care about how they impacted the rest of the team. They also didn't care about how they impacted other departments. While that description may not be "withdrawing" in the strictest sense, the lack of concern they described could certainly be a warning sign about a person who is either prone to withdraw or experiencing the depersonalization factor of burnout.

For those who like to daydream, this can be an especially dangerous trap. While there is nothing wrong with imagining different possibilities (because after all, leaders need to have a "vision"), when we find ourselves spending more time daydreaming that being engaged in our work or relationships, that has a real cost.

Depersonalized or Introvert?
This is also a good space to mention the idea of introversion. Just because someone is not "warm" does

not mean that they are depersonalizing. With the recent appreciation of introversion thanks to the work of Susan Cain and others,[1] I want to take a moment to distinguish between depersonalization and introversion. What we are talking about here is a noticeable change in behavior.

I tend toward the introverted end of the personality spectrum. Please understand, I like people. I really do. It's just that spending time with people takes energy from me rather than recharges me. So, sometimes I have to choose to be alone to rest and recharge. The way I guard against depersonalization is that I choose to withdraw for *a set period of time* so that I can then intentionally reengage later.

Intentional Influence: Strength and Vulnerability

I've seen depersonalization happen with leaders who tried to be collaborative and expressed vulnerability only to feel betrayed by their staff afterward. The developmental need is to lead with both strength and vulnerability knowing that in spite of our best efforts we will still either fail or be failed. How do we do this without becoming cynical?

When I coach on leadership, I often talk about "intentional influence." The basic idea here is that you are self-aware about your impact on the world, and you are taking intentional actions to achieve your leadership vision. One of the key supports for this kind of influence is ally and advocate relationships. This is because, to paraphrase leadership expert Barry Posner, "You can make a difference, but you can't do it alone."[2]

Let's define these terms and relate how that's important for beating burnout.

- Allies: those who run alongside you as you pursue your leadership vision.
- Advocates: those who speak up for you or provide additional resources when you need a spokesperson for you and your vision.

Remember how we talked about emotional exhaustion earlier? Well, these relationships will help you share the burden of the work you do so that you are not pulling the weight alone. That means it takes less energy to do the work. And, in order to have ally and advocate relationships, you can't continue to withdraw (depersonalize) from people, instead you have to intentionally engage them. When you are engaging in ally and advocate relationships for intentional influence, it means you get the double benefit of engaging with people and engaging with purpose (your leadership vision).

The Costs of Depersonalization
Under the best of circumstances, people do work that they find meaningful and work alongside people they feel connected to. When that happens, work is engaging – even energizing. With depersonalization, we find ourselves disconnected from meaningful work and meaningful relationships at work.

So, what happens?

- Ineffective teams
- Lack of community for self also means an underdeveloped support system
- Lack of fulfillment at work.

When you feel a lack of fulfillment at work, how do you show up at home? Let's talk about how depersonalization can impact your family. As mentioned earlier, being engaged with a family demands energy and intentionality. When my clients are struggling with burnout related issues, they find themselves retreating when they get home instead of engaging. They report being so pulled between work demands and home demands that they can't satisfy the demands of either (and we will talk about ineffectiveness later) and sometimes they anesthetize themselves against that feeling by relying on numbing behaviors after work rather than relationships.

I'm not saying a glass of wine at the end of the day means you are depersonalizing. However, if you find yourself using alcohol as a way to escape, then we have bigger issues that need to be addressed.[3] In its later stages, those struggling with burnout often self-medicate with alcohol or other substances. That's why it's so important to intentionally move the needle *away* from burnout and toward its opposite.

WHAT'S A HEALTHIER ALTERNATIVE?

Knowing what you want is important. Being able to articulate the opposite of depersonalization gives you a handle on what to work toward. Knowing what we don't want is good. Knowing what we do want is even better.

In my work with clients and conference attendees, I have people tell me what the other end of the spectrum is for them regarding depersonalization. They offer up options like:

- Pursuing people
- Not seeking distractions
- Offering praise instead of criticism
- Staying curious
- Focusing on the heart of the person instead of just their behavior
- Being open and vulnerable
- Not being critical when delegating
- Investing in energizing friendships
- Being open to new relationships
- Making time for people
- Experiencing less conflict
- Feeling the need to connect
- Being purposeful and engaging
- Being more curious around people

- Saying "I want to do this"
- Connected
- Attached
- Passionate
- Understanding
- Compassionate
- Expressing forgiveness
- Having community
- Not being defensive with people, but willing to engage.

Reading about concepts is helpful, but even better is relating in real life. What is the opposite of depersonalization for you? What is the healthier alternative you seek? The more clearly you envision the ideal state, the more likely you are to get there. When you can clearly describe it, it is easier to achieve it.

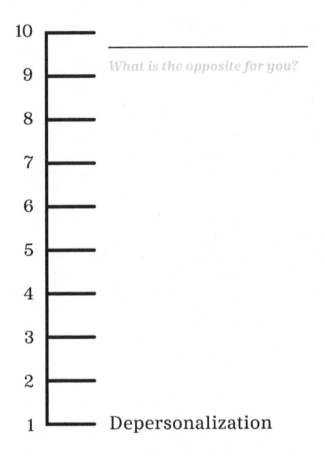

SMALL EXPERIMENTS FOR GETTING THERE

Ben was struggling at work because of a downturn in his industry. He was naturally a hard worker and he cared about his company – both as an operation and as a set of relationships with coworkers and colleagues. That's one reason that going through layoffs because of the downturn was especially difficult on him. Ben felt himself withdrawing from his colleagues and was quick to anger. These responses made sense given the demands of the situation, but they were getting in the way of his professional effectiveness and he was taking the stress from work home with him. If he wasn't careful, he wasn't fully present when at work and he wasn't fully present when at home. Moreover, he needed to go into the post-layoff season with deeper relationships that could handle the demands placed on a smaller team. What could he do to reconnect?

Since our focus is on beating burnout for yourself, your team, and your family, these experiments focus on the human relationship dynamics where we may be tempted to withdraw. These experiments will serve you well both in the workplace and at home.

Experiment #1 – Choose *Comedy* Instead of *Tragedy*.
Before earning a PhD in leadership studies and going on to become a leadership coach, I taught history and English classes at a local high school. During that time, I took summer classes for teachers that focused on teaching tragic and comic literature. One takeaway from those classes was that the basic difference between a comic story and a tragic story was how the story ended. Tragic stories ended in isolation (such as suicides and exiles) and comic stories ended in community (such as weddings).

I encourage my clients to live a comic story – one that is built around community.

Meg was dealing with a difficult relationship. One day she felt like the final straw had been snapped and she wanted to simply stop communicating with the other party indefinitely. As soon as she had that thought, Meg reflected on the comedy versus tragedy choice and realized, "If I do that, I'm choosing a tragic story. I don't want that. I want to live in community." So she did the hard work to address the frustration and rebuild the relationship.

When a coaching client sets a goal, I will sometimes

ask, "Who can help you with that?" I do that for two reasons: (1) By involving someone else as an ally or advocate, the client gains additional resources and even accountability outside of the coaching relationship for that goal. (2) By intentionally connecting the leader with another human being, they choose a comic path toward community as they pursue the goal. Put simply: community matters.

In one coaching project, I worked with several managers in a large organization that was spread across several sites. One thing that struck me about these managers is that they rarely consulted with peer managers about issues they were facing or reached out to each other simply to build a better professional relationship. I encouraged them to start intentionally connecting with their peers. While not all the managers were comfortable with this approach, those who did reported noticeable improvements in regulating their own negative emotions and how they dealt with stressful situations as a team.

Experiment #2 – Choose *Influence* Instead of *Control.*

For those high-D personality types (those motivated by a high drive for dominance, achievement, and competition), this can be especially difficult. If this is you, you probably have been greatly successful because of your ability to control outcomes. You most likely are a great competitor, used to being the best in whatever you tackle and always winning the prize.

Here is the problem. There are a lot of things we can't control in life. Here is just a short list:

- The weather
- The economy
- Our employees
- Our volunteers

- Our family members

As pointed out by Margaret Wheatley in her book *Leadership and the New Science*, there are very few things we can actually control – the best we can hope for is influence.[4] She explains that we live in a world where it's difficult to determine direct cause and effect. So instead of highly structured systems that focus on control, we are better served by networks that focus on influence.

In a variation of the theme of influence vs. control, *The Art of Possibility* by Rosamund and Benjamin Zander explains that when there are difficult things in life we can't control, the one thing we can control is how we relate to the situation or the person.[5]

So, high performer, stop trying to control everything and everyone. It only makes you resent them when they don't do what you want – or they will resent you for your micromanaging. Choose how you relate to people or to problems. Choose influence instead of control. For my highly driven clients, this is especially freeing.

Another client, Larry, had just stepped into a senior management role in his organization. He quickly found himself working seven days a week (a tendency he already had in his previous work that was now made more intense by his new responsibilities). Larry prided himself on being the "go to" guy before, and being in the middle of everything. Now that he was responsible for even more staff and operations, he was drowning in it all.

In one coaching session we hit upon a metaphor that shifted this for him. He said he felt like a soccer goalie who was responsible for every score against the team, and that he, personally, had to protect the goal. I challenged him to realize that in his new senior role, he needed to be the coach. It was no longer his personal responsibility to stop every shot, but rather he needed to choose and train the people who could do that.

The light bulb went on for Larry and he also felt

relieved to know that in fact he had a choice. Choosing to influence rather than control lifted the burden. The same goes for choosing comedy and community rather than tragedy and isolation. *You* get to choose.

Experiment #3 – "Here's What I Need from You. What Do You Need from Me?"

I often begin coaching programs with the Thomas Kilmann Conflict Mode Instrument.[6] It's a helpful tool for identifying a person's primary communication style in a conflict situation. As pointed about by the instrument's creators, there are two factors at work in any conflict situation: (1) "concern for self" which I call "my agenda," and (2) "concern for the other" which I call "your agenda." So, when it appears that my agenda and your agenda are at cross-purposes, we have conflict! (Even when we just *think* they are at cross-purposes, we feel conflict.)

The first step to resolving this impasse is to get really clear on your agenda and the agenda of the other person. The simplest way I know to do that is to use this formula when communicating: "Here's what I need from you. What do you need from me?" Once you've clarified that, both parties can then decide what they are willing and able to provide for the other person. Can't deliver on what they ask for? No problem. Offer an alternative that you can live with.

I also appreciate the concept of a "designed alliance" from co-active coaching as an "assumption buster."[7] To help us be purposeful in our relationships, we can uses designed alliances both at work and at home. How do these alliances work? Essentially both parties communicate, "Here's what I need from you" and they agree to engage each other that way. This is not a formal contract. When the situation changes, the alliance can be revisited and revised as needed.

Here are some variations on that:

- "I need the report by Wednesday. If I don't have it by then, how would you like me to follow up with you?"
- "I understand that you want more freedom to make this decision. For me to be comfortable with giving you that, I will first need ..."

Keep requests constructive. When you tell someone, "I need you to stop being a jerk," that is not helpful. Just because someone avoids being a jerk does not mean they will deliver on what you need. To help bust assumptions, be sure to provide positive and concrete descriptions of what you need/want from people.

Experiment #4 – "You Are Not a Threat to Me."
Let's return to our discussion of fight or flight. If we perceive that someone, such as a micromanaging boss or a combative coworker, is a threat to us, we will naturally withdraw to self-protect. Sometimes our perception is accurate and other times it is not. When you feel yourself withdrawing as a protective mechanism, try telling yourself "you are not a threat to me" while looking at the person.

Alex worked in a service industry where he constantly interfaced with both the public and managers from other departments. He confessed to me a growing anger with both customers and co-workers because he felt like he always had to do whatever they asked. As we dug further into the situation, it became apparent that Alex felt threatened in each of these interactions. Our first step was to break the fight or flight cycle in his mind. Once he was able to recognize the physical signs that he was in a fight or flight state, Alex would then tell himself, "You are not a threat to me," while dealing with that person. When he was out of fight or flight, Alex could then begin the process of communicating, "Here's what I need from you. What do you need from me?"

To the extent that you are clear on your personal strengths, weaknesses, and liabilities, it will be easier for you to clarify what you need in a situation. I will explain how in the next chapter.

Experiment #5 – Beware of Fair.
Some personality types have a strong need for "justice" or "fairness." The problem here is that, well, life's not fair (sorry to sound like a parent here). There will always be people who seem to consume more from your work than they contribute to it. There will always be people who seem to get paid more than you for doing less work. If you aren't careful, you will get so caught up in perceived slights that you isolate yourself from your peers and your organization. Are you willing to blow up your organization or work relationships when life is not fair?

By the way, when you start to feel this lack of fairness in work or home relationships, that means it is time to revisit, "Here is what I need from you. What do you need from me?"

CHAPTER REVIEW
- Depersonalization includes a feeling of withdrawal and disconnect from work and from others.
- The costs include ineffective teams and a lack of fulfillment at work and in life.
- Small experiments for beating depersonalization include choosing comedy instead of tragedy, choosing influence over control, and understanding that others are not typically a threat.

FOR REFLECTION
- What did you discover about depersonalization?
- Which of the small experiments makes the most sense for you?

- How can you apply that for yourself?
- How can you apply that for your family?
- How can you apply that for your team?

NOTES

1. Cain, S. (n.d.). *The power of introverts*. Retrieved from https://www.ted.com/talks/susan_cain_the_pow er_of_introverts
2. Posner, B. (2014, Jan. 30). I can make a difference, but I can't do it alone. Retrieved from https://youtu.be/3cpLFFZsbWY
3. I feel obligated at this point to let you know that Alcoholics Anonymous is a tremendous resource if you are concerned about your drinking habits. You can see their website here: https://www.aa.org/. Similarly, if you have a family member who struggles with addiction issues, Al-Anon is a great resource https://al-anon.org/
4. Wheatley, M. (2006). *Leadership and the new science: Discovering order in a chaotic world*. Oakland, CA: Berrett-Koehler.
5. Zander, R., & Zander, B. (2002). *The art of possibility: Transforming professional and personal life*. New York, NY: Penguin Books.
6. Thomas, K. W., & Kilmann, R. H. (1974). *Thomas-Kilmann conflict mode instrument*. Tuxedo, NY: XICOM.
7. Kimsey-House, H., Kimsey-House, K., Sandahl, P., & Whitworth, L. (2011). *Co-active coaching: Transforming business, changing lives*. Boston, MA: Nicholas-Brealey Publishing.

CHAPTER 8

BEATING INEFFECTIVENESS

"I feel like I'm doing everything, yet accomplishing nothing."

IN THIS CHAPTER, YOU WILL DISCOVER

- What ineffectiveness is, what it looks like, and the costs
- What the opposite looks like
- Small experiments for beating ineffectiveness

INTRODUCTION TO INEFFECTIVENESS

The MBI uses the category of "low personal accomplishment" or "low personal efficacy." When this emotional state is high in a person, the MBI interprets this state as a sense of being "ineffective," and that is the term I prefer to use with my clients when using this model.

Much is written and said about being an effective leader. When a bright person starts to dim due to burnout, their effectiveness suffers. High achievers who feel ineffective take it hard; hence it is also an indicator of burnout.

"Stan, I feel like I'm doing 'everything' and yet doing 'nothing' well." I've heard some version of that statement countless times from both coaching clients and colleagues. In our "always on" culture that seems to value busyness as a status symbol, our to-do lists are rarely done. Add to that, the inevitable self-comparisons that accompany the consumption of social media. Thus, the gnawing sense of ineffectiveness is common and it is caustic.

Ineffectiveness can be incredibly discouraging. If you get a lot of your identity from your ability to get stuff done, then what does that mean about yourself when your productivity diminishes? Or, as is often the case for my clients, when you simply *perceive* that your effectiveness diminishes. Often the sense of ineffectiveness is tied to a sense of powerlessness – that you are facing a situation where you have few authentic choices that you can make.

For example, when I asked a client, Ben, about his progress on addressing challenges facing his organization, he said he felt like he was throwing pebbles at a freight train. Does that sound familiar to you?

What Ineffectiveness Looks Like

Let's return to the illustration of keeping your hand balled tightly into a fist. While it's a fist, its usefulness is limited. Sure, you can hit somebody with it, but that's about it (and hitting people is not going to help you with that whole depersonalization thing). So when you finally relax it, all the strength is gone and you still can't use it. And because you previously cramped your hand, you may also be experiencing pain while accomplishing nothing. Your hand is ineffective.

When you genuinely care deeply about your coworkers and clients, you naturally want to deliver a work product that meets their needs, so that motivates you to do quality work. Similarly, when you genuinely care deeply about your coworkers and clients, you will also make the extra effort to know them as individual people and consider their emotional welfare. You feel like Superman.

However, when your level of caring and effort is relentless, this superpower switches to kryptonite. For example, when you get feedback that your work product does not meet expectations, you may second-guess yourself and the value of your contributions at work. Also, caring deeply about others can make it difficult to have hard conversations because you fear hurting them. Yet these hard conversations still need to happen.

Here are a few self-diagnostics to help you see where you are at regarding your "ineffectiveness."

- At the end of the day, do you focus more on the parts of your to-do lists that are still unresolved, or are you able to recognize the value of what you did accomplish?
- If someone says, "You've handled this situation better than most," do you feel successful – that you can be proud of how you've handled yourself? Or, do you see this as a failure – that you *should* have handled this better than *everybody* else?

- Do you have the sense that you are leaning your "ladder of success" against the wrong wall?
- Do you feel like a hamster in a stationary wheel that is always spinning, yet going nowhere?

In my own battles with ineffectiveness, there seems to be two internal voices fighting for my attention. The first voice is that of "The Dreamer." This guy is actually helpful, because he sees new possibilities to do really cool things in the world. The Dreamer often points me to opportunities that other people don't see or genuinely consider. His is the voice that empowers my sense of vision as a leader at work and at home. His mantra: "Consider the possibilities here!" When you look at the self-diagnostic questions above, guess where he points my attention. When I listen to him, I feel hopeful, contented, and full.

The other voice is "The Screamer." His voice is louder than The Dreamer's. He constantly points out perceived threats along with accusations of incompetence. His mantra: "You can't do this." When you look at the self-diagnostic questions above, guess where he points my attention. When I listen to him, I feel threatened, empty, and hopeless. In a word: ineffective.

One of the reasons I am a coach is that I want to help people manage their own Dreamers and Screamers. Because when The Screamer takes over, he will push us toward burnout, even when we are doing good things in the world.

These two voices have been in my head while writing this book. Here is what they had to say:

The Dreamer	The Screamer
This is an opportunity to make a difference.	You'll never be able to finish.
Think about how great it will feel when this is done.	There is still too much left to do.
The work is worth the effort.	You don't know enough to write this.
You have a lot to offer here.	Others will criticize your work.
This book will help you connect with others.	People will reject you when they read this.
The workload is manageable when you are patient with yourself and the process.	You are going to screw this up.

When talking with clients about ineffectiveness in their own lives, this is how they expressed it:

- A possible disconnect from reality because of *perceived* ineffectiveness versus actual impact
- Going deaf listening to The Screamer, so that the only message I can hear is his
- I apologize for everything
- I constantly feel like I need to give more or do more, even during the most productive and accomplished seasons of my life
- Feeling like no one can do anything right and I am a martyr
- The things I care about don't matter in the "real world"
- Total lack of control

- Always falling short
- Despair
- Unappreciated
- No results
- Hamster in a wheel
- A growing sense of anxiety and despair

The Costs of Ineffectiveness

These dimensions of burnout are not just identifiers to see how you are functioning. When you give and give and give and go-go-go, you cannot sustain that pace. Your efforts backfire. The cost of ineffectiveness feels like a weight on the chest. Life feels heavy and you start to get that feeling of "why bother." The voice of your Screamer has drowned out that of your Dreamer. When you feel like you are hitting the wall, you experience the costs of ineffectiveness that include:

- Feeling powerless
- Feeling like a failure
- Constant pessimism
- Work seems meaningless
- There is nothing to celebrate

What's a Healthier Alternative?

There's also an opposite feeling. Knowing what that is for you helps pull you up. It allows you to see that there is light at the end of the tunnel. Certainly the opposite of ineffectiveness is effectiveness. How do you put that into words for yourself?

Some of my clients have offered up feelings and phrases of:

- Not being so worried about results
- Not feeling like a martyr

- A hopefulness that even during hard seasons of life, what I do matters
- Being joyful and content while still getting things done
- Feeling like I'm making measurable progress toward a specific and meaningful goal
- When my actions help people grow spiritually and be emotionally safe
- Success
- Progress
- Intrinsic sense of accomplishment
- Celebrating success
- Energized and joyful
- Having clear success metrics
- Being comfortable when not in control
- Figuring out what is really important and doing that

Knowing what you are striving for can give you the first whiff of new motivation. What is your Dreamer saying now?

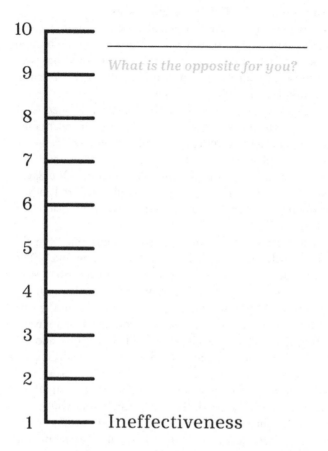

What is the opposite for you?

10
9
8
7
6
5
4
3
2
1 — Ineffectiveness

SMALL EXPERIMENTS FOR GETTING THERE
In the same way that we've considered small experiments for addressing emotional exhaustion and depersonalization, we will now consider ways to address ineffectiveness. While all of the experiments in the book are helpful "go-to's" I use when working with clients, I've found the following experiments to be especially helpful for me personally.

Experiment # 1 – Celebrate Successes.

This is one of the simplest small experiments that I can suggest, and yet I've seen it pay off time after time both at work and at home. Large or small, honor your successes and those of your team. You can begin this experiment in the workplace or with your family.

Years ago I read a book by Ken Blanchard called *Gung Ho*.[1] In it, he talks about the importance of celebrating success. During that time, one of our daughters was going through a phase where she resisted her mom and me constantly, and everything seemed like a battle. One day, I asked her to do something and internally prepared myself for the fight. When she smiled and replied "Ok, Daddy," I was stunned.

The snarky side of me wanted to blurt out "Finally! You actually do what I ask without fighting me." The better side of me chose to celebrate success. So I said, "That deserves a nickel!" I went on to explain to our seven-year-old that whenever I saw her do something that exhibited our family's values, we would celebrate it by putting a nickel in the nickel jar. When we had enough nickels, the whole family would go out for ice cream. Moreover, anyone in our family could "call a nickel" whenever they saw someone in our home do something that was especially good. The only catch was you could only "call a nickel" for someone else; you could not call out your own successes. With that small experiment, the tone in our home began to change as all of us began to watch for and celebrate the successes of each other.

Celebrating success at work does not have to be a nickel jar nor does it have to be an expensive party that is Instagram worthy. I've worked with some organizations whose version of "that deserves a nickel" was to stop in the middle of a meeting and say, "That deserves a fist bump."

Celebrating success can have a kind of snowball effect as "success breeds success." People are energized by those early, small successes and that gives them the confidence to tackle other larger projects, as well as point out the successes of those around them. One client, Martin, experienced this snowball as he began to delegate more to his management team – celebrating what they were accomplishing – which then gave him more time to do the strategic work needed as a senior leader.

Experiment # 2 – *Satisfice* Instead of *Maximize*.

In recent years, the idea of optimizing or maximizing *everything* has become in vogue. These tendencies, with their inevitable sense that "I'm not doing enough" lead to feelings of ineffectiveness and burnout. To move away from burnout, we have to understand the difference between doing what is really necessary and "over delivering" like Jimmy Big League.

In wrestling with this struggle, I've found the concept of "satisficing" to be helpful. I first discovered this concept from Gretchen Rubin's (the author of *The Happiness Project*) blog, asking "Are you a maximizer or a satisficer?"[2]

- Maximizers tend to obsess during the decision-making process, continually searching for the best option. They tend to be perfectionists, always looking for the best option, and as a result, they also tend to be less happy with their decisions. Maximizers habitually spend more energy than is necessary in order to make their decisions.

- Satisficers look for the "good enough" option (similar to the "minimal effective dose" we discussed earlier). And so, they expend the minimal amount of energy needed to make their decisions.

I recently purchased a new bicycle because I live near a bicycle path and I wanted to start riding again (after giving up mountain biking). Because I easily fall into the maximizer tendency, I could feel the drive to start researching multiple sites for determining the best bicycle at the best price with the most options, etc. Thankfully, I was able to snap out of that bottomless pit of worrying "is it good enough?" and come up with my minimal effective dose.

- I wanted a bike that would allow me to ride the local bicycle paths.
- I wanted a bike in a certain price range.
- I wanted to buy it from a local shop, because I wanted to make bicycling about being part of the local community as well as about exercise.

When I walked into the local shop a few weeks later and found that an entry-level bike that met all those criteria was on a close-out sale, I bought it with a big grin on my face. No looking back.

One irony here is that maximizers often do achieve better measurable outcomes than satisficers, yet they are less satisfied or happy with those outcomes. So when working to beat ineffectiveness, ask yourself if you are a maximizer or a satisficer, because maximizers will be more prone to feeling ineffective than satisficers – even if they are doing good work!

Here's an analogy I use with clients of what maximizing feels like. When I'm working to achieve a goal, I often feel like a pole-vaulter who has launched himself into the air. Holding onto his pole, and as he nears the bar and realizes that he can get over it, he thinks "Hmm … I can actually get over this bar. Well, if I can do that, it must not be challenging enough. So, I will try to hold onto my pole with one hand while reaching out to grab the bar and raise it higher while I'm still in mid-air and then see if I'm good enough to get over it." Crazy, right? Even crazier, when I share this illustration with the leaders I coach, they often say, "I know exactly what you mean." When we grasp that good enough really is good enough, we can beat burnout.

One way I help clients avoid ineffective maximizing is with the concept of "success metrics." For those who struggle with a tendency to over deliver, I work with them on the skill of clearly defining success with a short list of parameters. When those parameters are met, instead of jumping straight to asking, "what else could we improve?", we stop and celebrate success. Only after taking time to celebrate do we discuss opportunities for improvement. We do *not* try to move that pole vault bar higher while in mid-air.

Experiment #3 – Focus on Strengths. Correct Liabilities. Make Peace with Weaknesses.

At the heart of my coaching work is a process where we clarify strengths, weaknesses, and liabilities. Strengths are those things you are naturally good at and that give you joy. There are a variety of ways to identify these. For example, you can use assessments like the Gallup Strengthsfinder[3] or the VIA Character strengths inventory,[4] or you can simply ask people you trust for feedback about where they believe you are naturally talented. For the most part, we want to use our strengths to help us get things done.

However, none of us are good at everything. So, we have weaknesses. The trick here is to separate the weaknesses and the liabilities. Weaknesses are those parts of our life or skillset that are simply less than ideal. Liabilities are the weaknesses that hurt us. Those liabilities must be corrected.

Let me illustrate. Chris is not naturally good at math. Yet, as long as he can make sure that at the end of the month he has spent less money than he made – or in some cases, that the emergency fund has enough reserves to deal with unexpected extra expenses – then math skills are just a weakness. On the other hand, if Chris is not able to do the math necessary to keep from overspending month after month, then it is a liability.

Regarding weaknesses, we must learn to make peace with the parts of our lives that are less than ideal but not actual liabilities. In doing this, you may benefit from this prayer by Reinhold Niebuhr, sometimes called "The Serenity Prayer":

"Lord, grant me the strength to accept the things I cannot change,
The courage to change the things I can,
And the wisdom to know the difference."

Experiment #4 – Don't Take it Personally.

Raymond noted that every time he was in a meeting at a remote location, the body language of those present was off. People were distracted. Few smiled. Most looked upset. Usually Raymond was able to engage the room well, so this really threw his confidence. Some projects were struggling to make progress, and he decided that he must have done something to upset the team and lose their trust and respect. Raymond mustered up the courage to talk to a trusted colleague about this situation, confessing that he was having a hard time reading the room and asked if he had done anything to cause it. The response surprised him. "Don't take it personally. It's not your meeting that's the problem. It's the meeting right after yours that everyone hates." Raymond was relieved and able to show up with more confidence and make progress.

Speaking of not taking it personally, remember our earlier discussion of learned optimism? In his book *Learned Optimism*, Martin Seligman explained that one of the ways we challenge our perception of an adversity is to challenge our assumption that the adversity is pervasive, permanent, or *personal*.[5]

Sometimes we place burdens on ourselves that aren't ours to carry. This has been especially tough for me as an educator in both secondary and higher education. I want to see my students do well, and I do everything in my power to provide them with the structure and support they need in order to succeed. I constantly reevaluate my curriculum and teaching methods, and I gather feedback each term to make adjustments as needed. In spite of all that, some students don't do well. For one reason or another, they don't do the work. If I'm not careful, I can find myself stepping in as some sort of "rescuing hero," overextending myself (remember the Tai Chi example about what happens when we overextend?) and yes, burning myself out as an educator.

The simple fact is we live in a messy, confusing, complex, and ever changing world. More importantly, we need to "show up" in that world. Because things are so messy right now, it's the perfect time for you to show up as a better leader. The mess is not necessarily your fault (don't take it personally), but how you show up in that mess is your responsibility. This is another expression of "influence" instead of "control."

Experiment #5 – *Reflect* Instead of *Ruminate*.

We've already discussed the difference between "pressure" and "stress" according to the Center for Creative Leadership. I want to return to that difference here as we consider small experiments for beating ineffectiveness.

When we ruminate, we focus on our failures, our worries, and our worst-case scenarios. Ruminating is like only keeping score of your failures or possible failures while ignoring your successes. No wonder you feel ineffective! I've found from personal experience (because I tend to ruminate), that ruminating interrupts my body's processes of rest and digestion that are so necessary for me to be an effective and energetic leader.

As an alternative to ruminating, try "reflecting." Focus on present reality: what is working, what is not, and what you can do realistically in this moment. When we reflect, we ask ourselves what we can learn from our experiences and how to apply that moving forward. When we reflect, we check our assumptions. Are they accurate? Are they serving us?

CHAPTER REVIEW

- Ineffectiveness includes feeling like you are doing everything and yet doing nothing well.
- Pay attention to the voice of your dreamer more than your screamer.
- Small experiments to beat ineffectiveness include: celebrate successes; satisfice instead of maximize; reflect instead of ruminate; not taking things personally; and focusing on strengths, correcting liabilities, and making peace with weaknesses.

FOR REFLECTION

- What did you discover about ineffectiveness?
- Which of the small experiments makes the most sense for you?
- How can you apply that for yourself?
- How can you apply that for your family?
- How can you apply that for your team?

NOTES

1. Blanchard, K., & Bowles, S. M. (1998). *Gung ho.* New York, NY: William Morrow.
2. Rubin, G. (2006, June 29). Are you a satisficer or a maximizer? [Weblog] Retrieved from https://gretchenrubin.com/2006/06/are_you_a_satis/
3. You can find an online version by going to gallupstrengthscenter.com
4. You can access their survey at Viacharacter.org
5. Seligman, M. E. P. (2006). *Learned optimism: How to change your mind and your life.* New York, NY: Vintage Books.

CHAPTER 9

REINFORCING THE CHANGE

"Knowing how to bridge the gap creates hope."

IN THIS CHAPTER, YOU WILL DISCOVER
- A sense of completion
- A sense of hope
- A roadmap for next steps
- A benediction

WHAT I WANT FOR YOU

As we come to our final chapter, I am reminded of the advice from one of my mentor coaches: "Focus on what you want *for* the client instead of what you want *from* the client."

Yet given that I'm also wired to care deeply and work hard, I feel questions pop up around my own work like "Is this book good enough?" and "Will you like it?" I care about what you think, and I want to do a good job. However, if I just stay focused on that, I'm not able to serve you well. Moreover, these concerns are aligned with the voice of The Screamer who tells me I'm not good enough.

So I've got to focus somewhere else. I need to intentionally flip that felt need for approval (what I want *from* you) and focus on what I want *for* you. When The Dreamer thinks about this chapter, he envisions readers finishing the book with:

- A sense of completion
- A sense of hope
- Next steps
- A benediction

A Sense of Completion

Sometimes coaching sessions go amazingly fast. When that happens, I ask clients "do you feel complete?" That way I know they are confident that the dots have connected, they know what the next step is, and they believe it is doable.

My hope in this closing chapter is that you have a sense of feeling complete. Why? Because together we've:

- Identified what burnout is
- Considered what it looks like in our own contexts
- Examined three ways burnout expresses itself
- Discovered small experiments to push back against burnout

With that information, I trust you have a sense of (1) where you are now, (2) where you want to be, and (3) how to get there through the power of small experiments and reflective practice.

A focus on where you are now, where you want to be, and how to bridge the gap between the two are at the heart of coaching. When you've clarified these three things, you can move forward with hope.

A Sense of Hope

When we are in the middle of experiencing emotional exhaustion, depersonalization, and a feeling of ineffectiveness, hope is hard to come by. But remember, where we put our attention is where we will go. If we focus only on the exhaustion, then we may very well find ourselves stuck there. And even if we try to avoid it, there is no guarantee we will actually make progress toward something better. That's why we took time to think about the *opposites* of these burnout indicators and what that looks like in behavioral terms. Those concrete, observable behaviors give us a target of what to strive for and what to watch for in our lives.

Instead of focusing on "don't burn out," focus on reinforcing the positive behaviors you've developed through your small experiments. Focus on the path, not the obstacles. Remember: success breeds success. With each small win, you can be energized to take the next step.

NEXT STEPS: REINFORCEMENT

At this point, hopefully you've had numerous moments of clarity and are willing to try these small experiments to help you forward the action. You've also learned what it means to be a reflective practitioner, examining your experiences and finding new ways to apply what you discovered to deepen the learning and forward the action. If that is happening for you, congratulations! You are experiencing transformation. And because your transformation also benefits your team and your family, you probably aren't the only person to notice the change. Well done!

One of the challenges in making change "stick" is that once we get momentum on a particular change item, we tend to shift focus and move on to the next without setting reinforcements in place to keep the first change happening. This is one of the reasons that so many people are suspicious of change initiatives at work. Once the "shiny" wears off of the change program, things tend to return back to the way they were before. Let's make sure that doesn't happen to you when it comes to beating the three dimensions of burnout.

The way to make sure your changes for beating burnout "stick" is through reinforcement that continues to deepen the learning and forward the action.

At the beginning of our journey together, we discussed the ADKAR model for change. It's a helpful model because it is easy to remember (Awareness, Desire, Knowledge, Ability, Reinforcement) and because it clarifies where our change journey begins, and what it needs in order for that journey to continue successfully.

In this case, we began with an awareness of what burnout is and how it expresses itself in our worlds. We then asked you to imagine a different state that you wanted for yourself (tapping into what you desired). We also considered ideas and activities to help you get there (to address your knowledge and ability). Now it is time to think about how to reinforce our movement away from burnout and toward a way of living that benefits ourselves, our teams at work, and our families.

Reinforcement With Signs and Symbols

When I was doing my PhD work in leadership studies, I came across the idea of "symbolic leadership." What I mean here is that sometimes leaders use signs and symbols to influence an organization.

Think of symbols as a way to concretely express a big idea. For example, when a king or queen wears a crown, that bejeweled headgear is not very practical yet it is a reminder that this individual represents not just themselves but the presence of a nation. (That's why kings and queens use the royal "we" as they speak for more than just themselves.)

When I decided to refocus my coaching business, I also had to do the deeper work of refocusing myself. During that process, I started thinking symbols of who I wanted to be in the world both as a leader and as a coach.

Soon, one image came to mind: The Captain America Funko Pop doll. When I think of Captain America, I see him as a class act. He's a real gentleman who is respectful of people yet still knows how to kick butt when needed. That's who I want to be in the world. (Bonus: He has great posture, which is something I aspire to as well.) So guess who is sitting on my shelf, looking down on me when I work in my home office?

What symbols energize you, remind you to stay connected, and reiterate the idea that you do have personal power and can make a real impact in the world? Maybe you have a song instead of a symbol. For Brené Brown, she calls this kind of song her "arena anthem" – a song that pumps her up as she steps into the arena of life to face its demands.[1] Choose some signs and symbols to help you make your burnout-beating habits stick.

How to Make Small Experiments into Longer Habits

When working with leaders to bring new habits into their lives, there is one process that I find most effective: tie the new habit to an existing routine.

During previous health struggles, I lost a lot of muscle mass and upper body strength. I was frustrated by how weak I had become and the struggle was only intensified because not only was I lacking strength, I had little stamina, and I was still trying to work and take care of my family. The constraints I had to deal with were limited time, limited energy, and limited strength. Everyone has some version of these perceived barriers when dealing with their own challenges.

So start small. Incorporate one element into your existing routine. For me to regain upper body strength, I included some pushups in my daily routine. I decided that before I took a shower, I would do a quick set of ten pushups. At the time, it was all I had the strength for and ten pushups did not take a lot of time. After several weeks went by, I increased that 10 to 15, 20, 30, even 40 pushups a day before showering. Small, consistent, incremental action can achieve big and lasting results.

Dealing with Triggers

Aligning new behaviors with already established habits is one way to make positive change. We also must address our negative behavioral habits. How do we deal with those? Executive coach Marshall Goldsmith explains that dealing with triggers helps us break negative habits.[2]

What is a trigger? Triggers are those things that "set us off," activating our fight or flight responses. As we discussed earlier, sometimes those triggers are real tigers that deserve a fight or flight response. Other times, those triggers are just paper tigers that needlessly make us feel threatened and then expend both physical and emotional energy. In other words, triggers can be an example of a liability that we need to correct.

If you find yourself constantly in fight or flight, try this process:

- Think of a work situation where you were "set off" inappropriately.

- Visualize the situation. What happened right before you got upset? How did you feel? That event or feeling was your trigger.

- Now, come up with an alternative response.

- To take this to the next level, tell someone about the change you want to make. Ask them to give you feedback when they see you respond to the trigger. Let them tell you how well you handled the situation.

With that new awareness, you can manage your triggers. To do so, try this formula: "When [trigger] happens, instead of [old behavior], I will [new behavior]."

To show you what this looks like, let's return to The Screamer and The Dreamer. As you learn to navigate these two, look for the trigger that makes the Screamer sound off in your head. For me, any time I'm working on something new or ambiguous, The Screamer shows up loud and proud.

You can insert your own words into the formula but get used to noticing and managing your triggers.

To fight *emotional exhaustion*:

- "When I am overwhelmed with long lists of things that need to get done, instead of ruminating on the list, I will choose to find some part of the day to set my timer and intentionally disconnect."

- "When I feel my heart rate pick up, instead of getting more amped up, I will intentionally slow down."

- "When planning a busy week, instead of being overwhelmed by all I need to do, I will look for opportunities to include things in the week that recharge me."

To fight *depersonalization*:

- "When I feel hurt, instead of pulling away, I will ask myself if I want a comic story or a tragic story here."
- "When I feel threatened in a meeting, instead of reacting, I will first examine the tigers to see if they are real or paper."

To deal with *ineffectiveness*:

- "When I start a new project, instead of listening to the Screamer, I will choose to make space for the Dreamer. The Dreamer gets to talk first. The Dreamer gets to talk loudest. The Dreamer gets the last word."

Consider the application of triggers as an advanced example of Breathe and Big Picture (where you stop a minute and reconnect to what you really want here).

Working with a Coach

Of course, one way to keep burnout at bay is to work with a coach. I have worked with multiple coaches over the years to achieve a variety of goals. Working with an International Coach Federation (ICF) certified coach will provide you with reinforcement from someone who is trained to help you clarify the real change you want to make and walk with you as you make those changes.

In fact, I worked with a writing coach to get this book done. She told me, "You can write with ease and joy." I came to her because my family had previously bemoaned my grouchy attitude while writing and editing an academic textbook, and I didn't want that to be their experience with this project (or mine). Indeed, it would be a bit hypocritical for me to burn myself out by writing a book on burnout, becoming exhausted, disconnected from family, and feeling less than effective.

Knowing that I was writing a book on burnout because, well, I'm predisposed to experiencing it, I explained to my writing coach that one of our success metrics would be if I could complete the project without becoming "grumpy Stan." With my coach's help and feedback from my family, I'm thankful to say I recognized when I was in that mode and made changes.

Here are some of the things that I discovered during the writing process:

- I tend to assume that if something comes easy, it doesn't count.

- With patience, I really can write a book with small, focused blocks of time per day. That means I can write a book while also working, coaching, and enjoying my family – and yes, also sleep at night.

- When I follow my own coaching advice about "small experiments" and such, things really do go better.

- When I focus on offering a service for others rather than proving myself, it takes the pressure off.

As you try the small experiments in this book, people will notice, especially if you are brave enough to share what you are working on. They can learn from your example. Not only are you beating burnout in a way that your team and family will benefit, but when you provide an example and share with them what you learn, you can help them beat burnout in their own lives as well. Powerful stuff!

Please note that coaching is not a substitute for therapy. If these small experiments don't provide relief, I encourage you to see a licensed professional counselor.

A Final Experiment Set
As part of my own "comic" journey toward community instead of isolation, I'm part of a small group at my church. One member of that group is a professional counselor. When one of our group discussions turned to the struggles of fighting anxiety and depression, he gave all of us some advice that can also help you beat burnout.

"Each day, do something necessary, something meaningful, and something fun."

Let me break that down for you:

- When you do something "necessary," you have measurable proof for yourself that you are not completely ineffective. You got something necessary done!
- When you do something "meaningful," you fight depersonalization, which can occur when our lives are out of tune with our core values.
- When you do something "fun," you help recharge your internal engine so you can beat emotional exhaustion.

Choose each day to do something necessary, something meaningful, and something fun.

CHAPTER REVIEW
- "Reinforcement" will help you beat burnout.
- Different kinds of reinforcement include using signs and symbols, transforming small experiments into longer habits, dealing with triggers, and working with a coach.

FOR REFLECTION

- What did you discover about reinforcement?
- Which of the "next steps" makes the most sense to you?
- How can you apply that for yourself?
- How can you apply that for your family?
- How can you apply that for your team?

NOTES

1. Brown, B. (2012). *Daring greatly: How the courage to be vulnerable transforms the way we live, love, parent, and lead.* New York, NY: Gotham Books.
2. Goldsmith, M. (2015) *Triggers: Creating behavior that lasts – becoming the person you want to be.* New York, NY: Crown Business.

A BENEDICTION

I'm a bit of a word nerd. I think Latin and Greek roots are cool. So please allow me to share some of the language roots for the term "benediction."

"Bene" is the Latin word for "good." "Dictus" refers to "speaking." A benediction is literally, "good words," or words of blessing. In the Christian tradition, many churches offer a benediction at the close of their services as they send attendees back out into the world.

Likewise, I want to close my book with a sort of benediction for you, offering good words to encourage you as you go back to leading yourself, your family, and your coworkers.

On the following page is a poem shared with me when I was burning the candle at both ends as a student leader in high school. It spoke to me when I was 16, and I still find it relevant today.

"Don't Quit" by John Greenleaf Whittier

When things go wrong, as they sometimes will,
When the road you're trudging seems all up hill,
When the funds are low and the debts are high
And you want to smile, but you have to sigh,
When care is pressing you down a bit,
Rest if you must, but don't you quit.
Life is strange with its twists and turns
As every one of us sometimes learns
And many a failure comes about
When he might have won had he stuck it out;
Don't give up though the pace seems slow—
You may succeed with another blow.
Success is failure turned inside out—
The silver tint of the clouds of doubt,
And you never can tell just how close you are,
It may be near when it seems so far;
So stick to the fight when you're hardest hit—
It's when things seem worst that you must not quit

With burnout, you are forced to "quit" because your body doesn't give you an option. So instead of "rest if you must," I suggest changing the line to "rest because you must or you will quit."

Can you beat burnout? Absolutely. You have already taken the first step. I look forward to hearing your success stories. Please feel free to share them with me.

Thanks for reading.

ABOUT THE AUTHOR

Dr. Stanley J. Ward strengthens leaders so they can strengthen others. He does this as a leadership educator, writer and coach.

As an educator, Dr. Ward Dr. Ward has developed and taught a variety of classes for traditional students and adult learners. He is also a frequent presenter at the International Leadership Association's global conference.

As a writer, he has contributed to fiction and non-fiction projects for children, teens, and adults as well as co-edited the textbook, *Ethical Leadership: A Primer*.

As a coach, Dr. Ward is certified by the International Coach Federation and specializes in helping high achievers experience success both at work and at home. His clientele include senior leaders in industries as diverse as aerospace, automotive sales, financial planning, landscape architecture and various nonprofits.

Find out more and contact Stan by visiting stanleyjward.com or coachingforinfluence.com.

Made in the USA
Monee, IL
16 June 2024

59531996R00073